Spotlight on me

A GUIDE TO GIVING GREAT INTERVIEWS
AND
COMMANDING MEDIA

RAECINE WILLIAMS

Copyright © 2020 by Raecine A. Williams

All rights reserved. This book or any portion thereof may not be reproduced or used in any manner whatsoever without the express written permission of the publisher except for the use of brief quotations in a book review.

First Printing, 2020

ISBN (Paperback): 978-1-7364694-1-5

ISBN (Ebook): 978-1-7364694-0-8

Island Heart Press

Los Angeles, CA | Kingston, Jamaica

www.Raecine.com

For my parents,
the greatest on earth, and my fearless siblings.
Thank you for your endless support,
always inspiring me,
allowing me to chase my dreams,
and supporting all my crazy ideas.

For my best friends,
my cheerleaders, my champions.
Thank you for never letting me quit
and always reminding me of my why.
For being Never Too FAR.
For World Adventures.
For Thursdays.

CONTENTS

Introduction		7
PART ONE - PRESS PLAY		**17**
1.	Meet the Press	19
2.	Pitching to the Press	37
3.	Notice ME	55
PART TWO - INTERVIEW ACADEMY		**69**
4.	Ten Press Preparation Tips	71
5.	Let's Get Physical	89
6.	Breaking Bad (Habits)	111
7.	The Interview Itself	127
8.	Negative Press	139
PART THREE - HAPPILY EVER INTERVIEW		**155**
9.	Do as the Stars Do	157
10.	Spotlight Swag	171
It's a Wrap		187
Acknowledgements		189
About the Author		191

Introduction
"It's Yours Now"

"I have to go," the producer said hurriedly to me, handing me a stack of papers as he walked away. "Just get this done." I stared at him, waiting - hoping - for further instructions, but he was already in the distance.

It was the middle of a scorching July in Jamaica and I was a 17-year-old intern, standing in the middle of a television station with scripts in hand and no clue what to do next. I'd known I'd wanted to work in the media industry since I was 5 or 6, but with college approaching, I had taken on this internship to try to narrow down exactly what I wanted to study. Except *this* was not how it started. I'd worked at this station as a kid, starring in a children's series that was novel for its time. When I got the internship, I was outrageously excited, expecting all the fun and glamor I remembered from being on a set as a child. Instead, on my first day, I was shown to a tiny, windowless, dark room with a small, old television, an endless stack of media storage tapes, and a yellow legal notepad with a pen that didn't work. My job that summer was to log time codes from the tapes.

I was bored at hour one, miserable by hour two. A week in, I was ready to quit. I complained to my mom, who encouraged me to hang in there and keep showing up. If I really wanted to get somewhere in the industry, I was going to have to learn everything and be prepared to do some dirty work, she said. She was also working at the TV station that summer as a sports analyst, and even though it was a drag to drive in early with her, it was my extreme pleasure to peek into the studio to watch her work. By midday, mom would go home and I would revert to logging my tapes in misery, every so often nosing around the actual production I was assigned to, trying to be helpful in the hope that someone would notice me.

One early morning on my way to peek in at mom, an executive producer stopped me in the hall and asked how busy I was. Hesitant to confess I was wasting time before returning to my torture chamber, I told her I was just wrapping up helping on a production.

"Great," she said. "We need some help on another shoot."

It took me about a quarter of a second to say yes, my feet shuffling behind her before my brain even processed what I was doing. Even if it were just for the day, I would escape my logging and get to see another side of the TV industry. The shoot she needed help on happened to be for the show I'd been logging for - A scripted summer children's series involving 5 – 10-year-olds who reminded me of my role just a few short years before. They didn't have a production assistant, so my job that day was to do whatever the producer asked. I wrangled kids, printed scripts, escorted guests onto the premises, organized lunch, and even eavesdropped in glee on the gossip in the makeup room, as I waited for the kids to get done. It was the most exciting 8 hours of my entire life - and that's not an exaggeration. This time, I was in love on day one.

Two of the crewmembers, Aubrey the audio engineer, and Wedderburn on camera, were actually guys I'd worked with on the children's show I'd starred in years before, so it felt like home. When I was invited to assist the producer again the next day, I was elated. The executive producer called me in again a few days later to ask if I'd like to be an *official* production assistant, complete with (modest) pay, I was ecstatic and grateful I'd listened to my mom and kept showing up. I arrived early with mom every day for my duties as a PA, asking her to pick me up as late as possible. I offered suggestions, did any and all odd jobs, and still even logged tapes when my replacement intern fell ill. This time, I applied myself with the enthusiasm of a lab rat chasing cheese and odd fruit around a maze.

On the morning I'd been left standing in the sun with my sweaty palms slowly soaking the stack of papers I'd been handed, I was about to be officially initiated into the media industry. The producer needed to tend to a family emergency halfway through the shoot, and he'd left the whole thing in my hands. I turned to Aubrey, as he smirked with the boom in his hand. I must have had either a bewildered look in my eye or one begging him to tell me what to do, because before I could speak, his smirk turned into a smile as he gently shoved me forward and said "It's yours now."

That day was the beginning of an amazing summer, my introduction to becoming a producer, and the start of my wild ride in the media business. With Aubrey's cool help and Wedderburn's expert advice, I completed the rest of the shoot with 2 kids, and without any real training. It was exhilarating. When I was again called into our exec's office a few days later and asked if I wanted to be a full-time producer for the children's show for the summer – she'd heard excellent things – I immediately said ***yes***.

I was really lucky that summer, as I've been many times throughout my career, to have a ton of people to lean on. Together with Lori, another producer my age, I got to produce the kids' show plus help out on the "big" shows, the ever-popular Entertainment *Report*, and the live morning show, Smile Jamaica. We got to meet Shaggy and a few other celebrities that summer and my fascination grew and grew.

Lori and me with singer Shaggy while producing circa 2007

Within a little more than a decade after that summer, I'd go on to get a degree in film and creative writing, another in journalism, produce stories at the White House, write for magazines, work for newspapers, work on camera – scripted and unscripted, as well as actually produce the same morning show I was so excited to help on (Lori, too!). Better still, I got the opportunity to host and report for Jamaica's top entertainment show for 3 and half years under the tutelage of our island's best producer, eventually making my way to the red carpets of Hollywood, speaking to stars and covering entertainment on a daily basis. With every experience that was unfamiliar, or even frightening, I could hear Aubrey's voice in my head. "It's yours now."

If you're getting prepped for the next level of your business, brand, career, or life and you're worrying you may not cut it, or you're starting from scratch and you don't have a clue or maybe you've done this all before but you need to get better, fret not. Remember, no matter your age or stage, *"it's yours now!"*

It Matters

Do you know what almost every entrepreneur, actress, pageant girl, social media influencer, top athlete, artiste, brand ambassador, and CEO I've interviewed had in common? If you thought remarkable topics or natural charisma, that's not it. What all those folks had in common was **fear**.

A fear of a thousand people laughing at them in the comments of a digital story.

A fear of being misrepresented in a game-changing newspaper article.

A fear of a still from their TV interview becoming a meme that lives forever on the Internet.

A fear of sounding like an idiot.

And for all those people, it's a completely rational fear. Media representation can make or break you. In this digital age, most things never go away. One thing's for sure, it feels hard to get seen when you really need the media attention; but it's also extremely difficult to get *unseen* if things go wrong. One inappropriate word or sentence could inflict serious damage on your brand, your business, your image, and your reputation, or even end your career. Especially if you're a millennial, you know well that 'cancel-culture' is a real thing.

We've seen how this plays out in the celebrity world: Megan Fox comparing her director, Michael Bay, to

Hitler; John Mayer referring to his relations with Jessica Simpson as 'sexual napalm'; Miss Teen South Carolina bombing her response to why a lot of Americans can't locate the US on a map; Charlie Sheen 'winning'; and my personal favorite, Kanye West letting us all know that 'slavery was a choice'. Most of the above interviews inflicted some kind of reputational damage. All of these moments live in infamy on the Internet.

Now, these examples may seem a bit dramatic, and some of them even in character for their respective personalities, but the point is: these blunders will haunt them.

You may be thinking, "If I screw up a TV interview, maybe no one will even see and if they do, will they even care?" Maybe you think, "I'm not famous enough for my blunder to go viral." Maybe not, but remember when UK Professor Robert Kelly's kid crashed his live BBC interview? If not, look it up. It's viral. Maybe you're even thinking 'well, any press is good press.' If so, congratulations, perhaps you don't have anything to lose, and perhaps this isn't the book for you. But if you think you could stand to benefit even an iota from your chance in the media, keep reading.

Whether you're young or old, looking to brush up on the skills you already have, or you're brand new to the game, it never hurts to have media training. In an age driven by all types of media, with new formats born every day, **this stuff matters**. We're not playing small, even if you're starting small in whatever your field is.

It matters when you're a small business owner trying to attract customers to your new space and the local paper calls for a feature. It matters when you've finally won the state pageant and a national TV station has decided to do a story on your platform. It matters when after 4 years of posting your covers on YouTube, your music finally goes viral and iHeartRadio wants you on one of their syndicated shows. It matters when your company wins an award for best culture and the podcast requests are pouring in for you, the CEO. It matters when after years of research and studies, CNN calls you to share your expertise on a live program. It matters when you've just won a medal or topped a championship representing your entire nation, and the reporter asks you, "What does this mean for you?" It matters when your grandma, or other family member phones to say they saw you on TV or heard you as they were driving and they're so proud of you. It does matter. And I know it does matter because I've been on both sides.

I've been the one giving a candid interview about my swimsuit line. I've been the entertainment reporter asking a Grammy-nominated musician a question they didn't like. I've been the one who didn't do my research for a TV feature. I've been the (short-lived, thank God) meme. I've been on both sides of the camera. Yes, I've also been like you.

So if you're ready to put your best foot forward, I'm here to walk with you. The bad news: a lot of this stuff will take time, patience, and practice. The good news: most of the things you perceive as your media obstacles can be overcome. The great news: most of what we'll do is actually a lot of fun and I've enlisted a few prominent media friends to give you their expert advice as well. Are you ready? Because when you turn the page, we'll officially be on the record.

The opening credits from one of my first on-air roles circa 1999. You're in good hands ;)

Part one

PRESS PLAY

Chapter 1
Meet The Press

> *The media's the most powerful entity on earth. They have the power to make the innocent guilty and to make the guilty innocent, and that's power. Because they control the minds of the masses.*
>
> – *Malcolm X*

Who is 'The Media'?

The media can either be your worst enemy, or your best friend. People have blanketed practitioners across the entire industry as 'The Media', and have held them responsible for everything from the rise of mass shootings to the public's fascination with and fear of sharks. We're easy to blame because our news, TV shows, podcasts, radio shows, newspapers and magazines are consumed by billions of people every single day and have traditionally been relied on for information and facts. Now, am I here to tell you that the negative press the press has received is all 'fake news'? No. But I will put my neck on the line and say that the majority of journalists out there strive to be fair, balanced and honest, even if --just like in every profession--there are a few bad eggs.

Before you can truly become 'trained', I must introduce you to the different spheres of the industry, and help you understand who we are so you may use the media to your advantage and understand what our expectations and ambitions usually are. Together, we're going to figure out how to work with all the different types of media, and which formats will suit you best.

The opportunities can be endless when you're an expert or influencer in your field. As a producer, I watched all sorts of people get roped in to do different types of mediums. Music experts would be brought in as guest judges for our local American-Idol-esque performance show, political commentators to give their two-cents on late-night news shows. I was even brought in as a guest on a local cooking show once, simply because I'm a huge foodie. All these mediums present different demands and their respective pros and cons must be carefully considered.

I want you to keep in mind that no matter what kind of journalist or press practitioner you encounter – left, right, good, bad – their mission is to either get a story or provide entertainment. To be specific, an interesting story, or valuable entertainment. At the end of the day, if you aren't giving them one of these, you probably aren't worth the press. Remember that as you go through this book.

If it wasn't obvious from my introduction, my favorite form of media is TV. My years working as an entertainment reporter, and my current field at the time of this book going to press, have been some of the most exciting and fulfilling years of my life. Those years, and the hundreds of interviews with brand ambassadors, athletes, artists and high profile people, were the inspiration for writing this book. Despite my passion for TV, my most recent media obsession is the world of podcasting, which I fell into by accident. If you had asked me a few short years ago if I could ever do a medium that was audio only, like radio or podcasting, I would have told you *hell* no. Why? Because I thought my looks were a contributor toward my media success. Because I thought my accent was too distracting to be part of a package. Because I thought that without visuals, I couldn't produce anything actually worth consuming. Those beliefs were all wrong and almost stopped me from exploring a dazzling new star in the media universe and expanding my skillset and talent. I don't want you to make the same mistake. Most people have a form of media that they are comfortable with, but don't count out any type because you think you 'can't,' or because you've set your value based on the thing you believe you're best at. Even worse, don't exclude any medium based on some imagined physical flaw. I can't tell you how many times I've heard 'I don't have a face for TV,' or 'I hate the sound of my voice.' As you'll learn later, your message, your mindset, and the methods I share will set you up for media success; however you must have an open heart when it comes to all forms of media.

With that said, it's time for your first (fun) activity! It's a quiz. Who doesn't like acing a good quiz! In order to guide you through each form of media, it is key to see where your strengths lie. Before you begin, make a note of the form of media you're most comfortable with right now. Off the top of your head, with the forms of media you're currently aware of, what type of interview would you want to do today, if asked?

I'll do my interview this way: _____

Awesome! Now let's get started.

WHAT IS YOUR MEDIA LANGUAGE?

1. What materials do you prefer working with?

    A. Schedules and large planning
    B. Imagination / Creativity
    C. People
    D. Numbers, figures or tech

2. What personal hobbies align closest with you?

    A. Reading, writing or puzzles
    B. Drawing or Filming
    C. Socializing & attending events
    D. Sports, news or politics

3. Choose the adjective that best describes professional you:

    A. Organized
    B. Artistic
    C. Persuasive and effective
    D. Innovative / Resourceful

4. What sounds most like how you'd approach a challenge?

    A. Write it out
    B. Brainstorm
    C. Talk it out
    D. Visualize alternative opportunities

5. What would you say is your professional weakness?

    A. Perfectionist
    B. Nonchalant
    C. Stubborn
    D. Dismissive

6. What type of learner are you (You may choose more than one).

    A. Visual
    B. Hands-on
    C. Aural (hearing directions and speaking answers)
    D. Auditory

7. What would you describe as your first impression on others?

    A. Knowledgeable
    B. Inspiring
    C. Confident
    D. Passionate

8. How would you describe your professional industry experience?

   A. Study-based
   B. Self-taught
   C. Industry immersion/networking
   D. Skills-based

Mostly A's: PRINT

Expressing yourself for translation to word form is probably an area you'd excel at. Organized people and perfectionists willing to cross T's and dot I's usually do great print interviews.

Mostly B's: EMERGING MEDIA (SOCIAL)

Social media is devoid of most rules and a place to truly explore new forms of communication. Your imagination would be perfect for this medium!

Mostly C's: VIDEO

Lights, camera, ACTION! Your personality lends itself to being on a screen. Video requires personality, charm, reading people well, and other attributes you likely have.

Mostly D's: RADIO / PODCAST

We're listening! Passionate, innovative and well-versed in facts and knowledge. You have just what it takes to make it with no visuals.

MY MEDIA LANGUAGE IS _____

Did your quiz result differ from your original answer or the form of media you felt most aligned with? If it *did*, take a look at your second highest score and pay attention to that form of media as your 'second strength' as we go along. If your results *didn't* match, take some time to think about why you've not considered this particular form of media and whether you have any biases against it. When I've administered this quiz to groups, traditionally, 90 percent of the cohort get a different result from what they *thought* would be their strongest alliance. This serves to show you that you may be more versatile than you think. Let's discuss a few things before we move on.

The Mediums

Although media's vehicles are ever evolving, there are a few staples that won't be going anywhere anytime soon. These are probably the ones that come to mind when you think about 'The Media', but all forms offer specific benefits. In its simplest form, we can divide the media into 4 categories: video, print, audio and what I like to call 'emerging' or 'millennial' media, which consists of social media and internet-based outlets. We'll discuss what's contained within each category, and the pros and cons of each. We'll also talk about how to directly tackle various forms of interviews on these mediums later on.

Video

Live Television

As the name suggests, live television is broadcasted to its audience instantly, or moments after a recording. There's usually no editing involved, save for certain places that use a slight delay to bleep out any foul language or oddities. Newscasts, morning shows, award shows and sports programs are often live. Live television was invented about 24 years before video was, so this was how people did it back in the day. With live TV, your message is delivered in real-time, and will usually be fresh, relevant and on-topic. These days, it's often accessible on the internet as well. Of course, live means there are no do-overs. What you said is what you said, and people will see it at that moment. Live TV interviews also usually have strict time constraints.

Pre-recorded Television

As its name also suggests, pre-recorded television segments are shot ahead of time, and usually edited, and packaged for TV. Most live newscasts and talk shows will usually contain pre-recorded packages. With pre-recorded TV, you're able to repeat things or do a few takes in a controlled environment that usually allows for better concentration, but be aware that your interview may be edited for content and clarity, which may sometimes remove some of your context if you were very lengthy. There's also no guarantee when it will air to ensure the timeliness of your content.

Shot Live Television

Now here's a sort of a tricky one. You may encounter television segments that are 'live' in the sense that they involve a live audience or other immediate elements, but they are not broadcasted immediately. These types of programs are usually aired within hours or days of shooting and are normally edited, but similar to live, there are no do-overs. A producer will have also organized all the details ahead of time. With these types of interviews you'll know what questions are coming and you'd have supplied pictures or videos to go along with these questions. Though you'll be better prepped, hosts for these shows still follow the lead of the conversation, leaving plenty of room for ad-libbing. With this type of TV, there's usually a one-on-one, and it's usually more intimate with light editing. Unfortunately, (or fortunately by the end of this book!) there isn't much room for do-overs. It may involve a studio audience or people watching.

Print (or Publications)

Newspaper

While many people consider newspapers ancient history, don't count out this form of media! Although newspapers don't fill the instant gratification a lot of us have these days; they're still regarded as one of the most reliable news sources around, especially smaller local papers. While online items technically live forever, there's still something special about having a newspaper clipping preserved. The bonus these days is that most items printed in a newspaper will usually be paired with a digital story. Newspaper journalists may call or meet you in person for your interview and it may involve a photoshoot, or they may ask you to supply photos. For newspaper interviews, you're able to repeat things and even clarify on most occasions, save for press conferences where your words may be edited for content and clarity and in some cases may lose its context. A newspaper interview also may not be published immediately.

Online Article

An online article is the internet version of a traditional newspaper article. Like the newspaper article, sources and journalistic accuracy are usually key, but unlike the newspaper, an online article can, and often will be updated if there is developing information or further resources. With online articles, the turn around is often very quick, so make sure you're checking for accuracy as you do have the opportunity to reach out post-publishing with clarifications.

Blogs

Most of us consume blogs at least once a week. Blogs generally live on the internet, but while most newspapers are traditionally businesses with several writers or journalists on staff, a blog is usually run by one or two people, with a smaller staff of writers. Blog posts are usually shorter in nature than a traditional newspaper article, usually involve less or no sources and may take on the voice or be more personally intertwined with the author. Blogs can make for a casual, fun interview or feature although some may not have the notoriety of a traditional media outlet.

Magazine

While newspapers provide fairly timely as well as evergreen content; magazine articles are usually not as timely as the content is generally planned in advance. Magazine articles offer a lot more room for visuals and are less to the point, with lofty descriptions and more substance to articles. A magazine article is a beautiful place for an impactful in-depth feature, but keep it evergreen since there is usually a gap in time until it goes to press.

Audio

Radio

Radio is one of the oldest forms of broadcast that is still exceptionally used today. While people get choosy with TV, getting rid of their cable and subscribing to streaming services or simply using the internet, radio is said to have a higher reach platform than TV, PC, tablet and mobile. Radio is live most of the time, so again, bring your A-Game since there are do re-dos.

Podcast

Podcasts come in both the recorded live, and edited form, and usually feature a host or hosts on a niche topic. Podcasts are a great place to reach a targeted audience and to expose your message to a new audience. Podcasts, especially ones with a smaller listenership can also be a great training ground for radio interviews and a great place to build your 'press section.'

Social Media Services (or Emerging Media)

Social media has transformed users from passive content readers into content publishers, thereby making their role more significant. As my readers who are influencers probably know, I would have to write a new book every week to keep up with the new forms of media on social platforms. From Instagram lives, to TikTok to Facebook Watch and beyond, creativity lives on here. While a lot of these platforms mimic traditional media, they each take their own twist, with some being far more informal, while others require subscriptions, certain time limits or caps. They border on the whimsy with filters and features. They're interactive with live feedback in the form of emojis, emoticons, comments and captions. If you have a dream for a crazy segment, there's probably a place for it within one of these platforms. If you find yourself offered a social interview you'd like to take up, be sure to buff up your profiles. For the sake of knowing what the possibilities are, let's take a look at the two general types:

Live / Streaming

Much like television, you are live and direct. Except, instead of a TV audience, you are on display to the internet, specifically to the followers / friends / fans of the owner of the live or the stream.

SnapShot

This is an interview conducted, whether via video, audio or print, that is specifically formatted for social. This may mean the story is abbreviated, animated, dubbed and more. For video, it may be shot video phone vertically or it may be professionally packaged ahead of time. Anything is possible on social, however it generally shys away from long form.

Interview Formats

Now that you know all the platforms an interview could take place on, let's talk a little bit about a few of the formats you'll find. It's helpful for preparation to know the format of your interview. Keep in mind that interviews can take place in person, where you are invited to show up at a physical location or where you find yourself in the same location as your interviewer. Alternatively, you may be interviewed remotely where you can call in via telephone, video in via Skype, or even send in written answers.

One-On-One

It's just you and your interviewer for this one! This can take place in person, or remotely.

Panel or Conference

Conferences usually involve other interviewees beside yourself, some of whom may be in person or remote.

Scrum

A scrum happens when you are the sole subject surrounded by a lot of reporters. This can take place in an 'expected' form such as on a red carpet or after a press conference, or it can be an ambush as detailed below.

Ambush

In an ambush, you have no idea the interview is coming and you may be stopped on the spot at an event or even while conducting your private affairs to be asked for an interview. We'll talk more about how to approach these later on in the book.

What makes a media source reputable?

We live in a world of biased journalism, questionable news sources and a lot of melee and mix-up. These days, anyone may call themselves a journalist and it's up to you to decide who broadcasts your message. When deciding what sources to reach out to, here are a few questions to ask:

Are they accurate?

Do they fact check? Is the writing free from spelling errors - from your email correspondence to even in the lower thirds of the names of their past guests? Are they citing sources and reporting information that is accurate or are there inaccuracies and frequent corrections?

Are they responsible?

Unless your purposely intended target is a gossip blog or a very right or left leaning publication--which does happen, is the source reporting responsibly with little bias and plenty of diverse sources? Do they have facts, or just hearsay? If they do stray towards gossip or a certain leaning, are they transparent about it?

So, which outlet should you target?

The outlet you target depends on the message you wish to share and what you have to offer that specific outlet. You'll learn more about what to offer in a pitch in the next chapter, but here are a few considerations to get you started:

Video	**Print**
- I have a vivid visual component - My physical presence is a part of my brand - I definitely want to be seen - I don't mind being edited - I mind being live - I don't mind an audience watching	- I would love something long form - I don't mind this being published further in the future - Pictures would be perfect - I want to be edited for clarity - My offering will be relevant for quite some time
Audio	**Social**
- I don't have a strong visual component - I have a lot to talk about or unpack - I have a strong audio component like my voice or music - I want to reach a very wide audience, quickly - I'd prefer not to be seen	- I have a lot of creative ideas - I want to reach a specific personality's followers - I want to reach a very specific audience, quickly - A short piece is fine with me - I want instant interaction or feedback

Chapter 2
Pitching to the Press

 People do not buy goods and services, they buy relations, stories and magic

– Seth Godin

The question I got the most, even before I started media coaching was "how do I get on your show?" Everyone wanted to know, whether for themselves, a friend, a client or a colleague. I didn't just get this question in my capacity as a producer either. I got it as a host, a production assistant, even just as a regular girl in a crowd. Aside from the questions, I've also seen my fair share of pitches - most of them were horrible, some of them hilarious, few were worth taking seriously.

It's a question I was hesitant to answer at first. After all, every producer is different, every show is different, every interviewee is different - how was I supposed to tell you how to get on somebody else's program? But the further on I got in my career, the more I realized that the fundamental art of pitching your story to the press is the same. Although there are internal considerations beyond your pitch itself that may make or break the decision, there are plenty of things well within your control that you can do to get yourself an interview. Someone once asked me what I looked for in a potential guest for the morning show I produced, and the answer is best told in a story.

Early into my producing role, I was charged with leading a segment called "Ten Minutes to Your Health." As the name suggests, it was a 10-minute segment and all about health. I'm not a big health buff and I struggled to diversify the content every week, especially within the parameters of our older, mostly Christian, mildly conservative audience. I made an effort to put more energy into "Ten Minutes to Your Health" and decided I wanted to do a segment on naturopathic and holistic health. It was something I thought would be beneficial for our audience, something a little different and hopefully informative - especially in a country where healthcare is not always readily accessible. I figured with such a big concept, I needed the right personality to capture people, so I started looking. I didn't want anybody too young and unconvincing, but no one too boring and stuffy either. Not surprisingly, naturopathic practitioners were not so easy to find, but I searched and searched until I came across a woman who we'll call Noor for the purpose of this story. Noor had a practice that was well reviewed, she had several articles published both by and about her in both of our national newspapers, she had a compelling story of how she ended up in this practice, and she was a Maroon, an early set of Jamaican people descended from escaped African slaves who established free communities in the mountains of the eastern part of the island. She was exactly what I had envisioned, so I called her up, and once I did, I was sold. "I'm a Maroon, you know," she told me, indicating she would be dressed as such in their traditional garments. *Great*, I thought. I spoke to Noor a few more times before the date of her live TV interview, and she sent me all the materials and information I requested.

On the morning of the show, Noor arrived early, dressed in a beautiful all-white garment with her head covered. I greeted her personally and escorted her to the make-up room, where I left our talented artists to it as I continued to prepare for the show. Noor's segment was about the third or fourth that day, and with a packed, exciting show that morning, I didn't get the opportunity to duck out of the control room and check on things like I sometimes did. Shortly before Noor's segment, I heard some commotion, but had to dash into the control room to deal with an issue before I could truly get into what the commotion was about. It didn't take me long to find out, however. By the time Noor was mic'd up and the segment had begun, a production assistant came in and asked me "Where did you find this lady? Are you crazy?" I didn't know what she meant. Why would I be crazy? I turned my attention back to the set, where Noor was explaining who she was and how she knew what she knew. My host challenged her. "So you believe in healing through natural medicine, or through potions," he asked her. *Potions?*, I thought. *Where was he going with this?* Noor answered the question and my host began to challenge her. About a minute later, I realized that he suspected Noor was a practitioner of Obeah, a type of spiritual practice around the Caribbean. This spiritual healing practice was thought of as taboo, especially to our audience. While I personally did not have any particular thoughts or biases against Obeah, or its practitioners, I knew it was something our audience would have a huge issue with. My host was now on a rampage with proving this woman to be an Obeah lady, completely contrary to where the segment was supposed to go and what it was supposed to be about. *"WRAP!"* I screeched into the headset. But it was too late, I'd lost control of my segment and my host and the entire crew was buzzing about the commotion earlier, which involved Noor and a one of our anchors, who happened to be a pastor, getting into an altercation involving a lot of "rebuking". My phone buzzed with a text message from my cousin. Is that an OBEAH LADY you have on Smile Jamaica? LOL!" When I finally got my host to wrap the segment, I was exasperated, and I'm not really sure how I made it through the rest of the show knowing the scrutiny that was to come. I rushed home right after, and didn't check social media or answer my phone for the rest of the day. The next morning in our all-hands production meeting, the first order of business was my show. A board member had called concerned. Viewers had written and called in, outraged. I received a lecture on what content and personalities were appropriate for our show - "didn't you screen this lady before you brought her on?". *I did!*, I insisted, but the truth is, Obeah or not, Noor brought to the table exactly what I was looking for as a producer. She checked every box. And what were those things? A humble brag, an example, action, and a personal touch - an acronym I've now come to use for pitching, called HEAP.

> **HEAP**
>
> **H** - Humble Brag
>
> **E** - Example
>
> **A** - Action
>
> **P** - Personal

Before I dive more into HEAP, I won't leave you hanging on the story. Noor's segment got me a whole lot of backlash, but we also had a fair share of our younger audience call in and ask for her contact information. People did pay attention and were captivated, even if it wasn't for the original reasons. The segment had everything I'd hoped it would have, just for the wrong audience. At the end of the day, Noor was a great interviewee and delivered on the HEAP that I got from her in the pitch stage. I spent the next few weeks with my content heavily scrutinized by my executive producer, but I commited to never having a boring segment ever again. So how can you have your HEAP and give your pitch the best chance of being accepted? Let's start with element one, the humble brag.

Humble Brag

What was Noor's humble brag? Noor's humble brag was that she had countless articles by and about her floating across the internet, giving her credibility. In fact, that's how I found her! She wasn't overplayed or sensationalized, but just enough to give her authority. When pitching, in order to sell yourself, you have to have a brag. You have to have a reason people will believe you. You have to have a reason people will trust you. You have to have a reason why you're the person who should share this information. At the same time, you don't want to come across as over-publicized or ostensibly self-promoting, so the brag has to be humble. Traditionally, humble-bragging is false modesty and can come across as insincere, but for us, the humble brag will serve to direct attention to our brand, product or service. Here are some good examples of things you can use for your humble brag:

- Material written about you
- Material written by you (and published!)
- Testimonials from prominent clients
- Studies or information that back up your cause

Be sure to pitch a different concept than the ones you're bragging about so the person reviewing feels that they are getting something fresh, original and still of as much value as others. For example if an article was run calling you the world's most knowledgeable florist, pitch an idea for a piece on sustainable flower businesses - you can work yourself in after!

Example

"I suffered for years until I turned to Naturopathy," Noor told me. "My son was sickly too. Other children stayed away from him until we started natural medicine," she said. She detailed the ailments that benefited from her practice and illustrated how persons were healed, giving me plenty of examples that I knew she could be asked about and discussed during the interview. Of course, having established her credibility through her impressive achievements - i.e. her humble brag - all these examples were golden to me, and I remember jotting down the best ones to put in the host's notes to ask her about. I want to know what your product can do, I want to know how your work affects people, I want all the details that set you apart - I want examples! This is the easiest part of the pitch for most people, but if it doesn't come naturally to you, ask yourself this question: How has my _____ (company, YouTube channel, medical practice, etc.) changed a life.

Action

While there is a fine line between action and example, the difference of detail is one that's likely to give you the edge when it comes to being selected for an interview. While an example or sample shows off what you or your product or personality can do, the action shows how you can apply it.

Now that you've illustrated how your offerings can help our audience, tell us how you're going to bring that example to life with action. It's so extremely important to have action of some kind no matter what medium you're using. Noor couldn't show me a physical example of her healing, but she wanted to bring a few of her natural products and use them on her son to demonstrate how they were applied. Whether it's a product, service or simply your God-given talent, offer it, even if it doesn't seem intuitive. Sure, I can't hear you sing in a newspaper article, but if you tell me that a professional singers warm up can be beneficial for preserving a teacher's voice, then offer to sing a few bars during our print interview. I'll certainly describe your voice in the article. If you get me involved to try it, I'm likely to write about that experience too. Say you're an athlete. While I don't expect you to do the 100m hurdles in my TV studio, if your example of success was your warm up, and you offer to lead me my host and two crew members through your signature warm up program, I'm that more likely to take you on. Show us why you deserve a spot, even if your offering doesn't seem obvious!

Personal

You've seen this a billion times on TV. An American Idol contestant telling you the story of how his house burned down and he had to start from nothing. The winner of a talent competition who overcame some of the challenges of autism to take the top spot. A teacher in a local school who appears on *Ellen* to be surprised with endless gifts and cash as a reward for dipping into her own pockets to make sure her students weren't hungry. These all tug at our heartstrings and pull us in because they get *personal.* But listen to this: You don't have to have a sob story or a tragic backstory of any kind to make your pitch personal. In Noor's case, she actually did have a compelling story as to why she turned to naturopathy. She'd been involved in an accident and was told she wouldn't walk again. But that wasn't the aspect we focused on. What made it personal is that she was a Maroon. She was part of a tribe of our country's earliest but somewhat obscure people. She dressed like them, she had intimate knowledge of their culture. For a country big on pride, this was personal. Challenge yourself to dig in - beyond a sob story even if you have one. What can people relate to with you? That's what a producer wants to hear.

Now that we know the HEAP we need, let's talk about *how* to pitch. Do you call? Do you send an email? A note by carrier pigeon? This is where each producer differs, but in my opinion, your safest bet is email. Producers and casting folk are usually busy people. Even if they pick up their phone, they may not have time to hear your whole pitch. I'm also a big fan of sending examples of your product if it's something physical. Who doesn't like getting free stuff?

Let's talk about guidelines for your email pitch:

Pitch Checklist

☐ *Professional email*

Let's start here. If your email comes from BarbieDollUniCornPrincx123@gmail.com, you've already lost. While you don't necessarily need to send your pitch from a company email, your address must be professional. Even if you're a clown, ProPartyClown@

gmail.com or even something snappy like Renee-ClownsAround@gmail.com is better than Funky-ClownGal680@gmail.com.

- ☐ *Correct Name*

    I can't tell you how many times I've gotten a pitch addressed to the name of my top competitor. Now I know two things about you: 1) That your attention to detail is poor and you'll probably be annoying to work with and 2) That you're probably sending out a mass pitch. Sending a pitch with the wrong name or outlet is an excellent way to annoy a producer and ensure I don't read further than the salutation. It's always great to check the spelling of a name too. There's nothing more irritating than reading my name spelled wrong when it's actually spelled out for you in my very email address.

- ☐ *Tailor your pitch*

    I don't expect you to craft a brand new message complete with new copy for every person you send your pitch to, but I do expect you to tailor your pitch to the person or outlet you're sending it to. If you're a designer and you know this station has a younger viewing audience, you'll perhaps choose to include visuals of your more flirty pieces. If you're a recording artist, and your radio interview is an older audience, you'll offer your example of a song they can relate to.

☐ *Short and Sweet*

I mean this in the nicest way, but we don't have all day to read your pitch. Get to it, and get to it quickly. Draw us in and tell us what it's about. A polite opening is, of course, awesome, but no need to overdo it on the pleasantries. There's no need to be overly formal either, but keep it respectful.

☐ *Catchy Subject Line*

When pitching you want your subject line to give information, but also you want to lure me to open it. You also want to do it in 10 words, or less, so this may be something you need to sit and craft. For example, if you're a makeup artist you could go with something like, "*Summer Beauty Picks by JLO's Ex Makeup Artist.*" You'll really want to think about what aspect of your HEAP you can bring out in this subject line.

☐ *Punchy First Sentence*

In this first sentence, you need to show me how I can serve your audience in an interesting way.

No pressure! Again, this is something you'd want to take a moment to craft, but it doesn't have to be hard if you've identified your HEAP. For example, if Noor had to send me an email, I would expect her first line to say something like, "I've been watching 10 Minutes to Your Health, and I think the way I've used natural medicine to heal people for the past 10 years would make for an excellent discussion on your Morning Show." You can then proceed to briefly introduce yourself and give me further details.

☐ *Contact Info*

Be sure to include a phone number or the best way to contact you.

☐ *Proofread and Spell Check*

Actually, do it twice. Typos hurt your credibility.

Spotlight Swag:
Check out a simplified version of this checklist as well as pitch templates in the last chapter of this book!

As I've alluded to before, your pitch is something that you want to take some time to craft and develop correctly. As a speaker, I have several templates of my pitch targeting different audiences and platforms, all with room to personalize. If you're finding it difficult to get your HEAP together, or craft your pitched details, not only can you check out the Spotlight Swag chapter of this book, but here's a fun exercise with a few funky scenarios to get you unstuck.

Instructions: Mix and match the following mediums, interview types and fictional scenarios to come up with a pitch. Don't forget your **HEAP.**

Medium	Scenarios
Radio	**Fishmonger Inc.** Fishmonger Inc. is a large fish retailer servicing hotels all over the country.
Television	**Broken Dolls Company** Broken Dolls fixes old toys, especially dolls, and re-sells them at a discount to children in need
Podcast	**Island Cat Cafe - Grand Opening!** The opening for a cat cafe where you can relax, have coffee and be surrounded by cats!
Newspaper Article	**Goat Mow** Goat mow will dispense goats on your lawn to cut your grass

Instagram Live Interview	**The 3 Grand Subscription** This subscription service sends you a random item from their inventory listed on their website every month. All items are valued above $30.
Blog	**Mannequin Viewing Day at Mannequin Co.** A foreign owned mannequin company is having a mannequin viewing day
Shot Live Talk Show	**Rent-A-Chicken** A company that provides you with a starter kit to raise a chicken in an urban backyard
Magazine Article	**Farrah Roofing Company** A roofing company that makes fire and waterproof roofs

Spotlight Swag:

Want more HEAP practice scenarios? Check out the Spotlight Swag chapter of this book!

Pitch Pitfalls

As I mentioned previously, there will always be elements out of your control that result in your pitch not being accepted. If you're following the advice above, you give yourself the best shot. However, here are a few instances that could cause your pitch to be rejected:

Boring

This automatically violates HEAP principles. If your topic is a potentially humdrum one, you need to be sure to find an interesting angle or aspect. I was once pitched a segment by a roofing company who wanted to… talk about roofs. That's it! No demonstrations, no added spice, nothing. Let's just talk for 10 minutes about roofs. I sent them straight to our marketing department who charged them an arm and a leg to have their boring conversation about roofs, which I'm sure nobody watched. This brings me to the next pitfall.

No Visual (or Auditory) Interest

I want to use this pitfall to emphasize the points in HEAP. Just because you have a tangible product or a physical demo, that does not make your pitch automatically interesting. If my roofing company above had offered to bring in samples of their roofing tiles, I'd likely still not be interested. If they brought in samples of their roof tiles and paint or water to put on the tiles to show their resilience or cleaning abilities or whatever, now you've got a bit more of my attention.

No Drama

Let's face it. We love drama. In this case, I don't necessarily mean make a scene, I just mean the audience can't automatically know what's going to happen next. So my tile company has their tiles, and their paint and water… Where's the drama? If they offer my hosts water and paint guns and challenge them to a competition where they spray the tiles randomly and turn the whole thing into a competition, they've got me.

Repetition

Yawn. We've seen it before. Sure it's action packed and visual, but doesn't every ____ company do the same demo or talk about the same thing in the same way? Take time to research media interviews in your same market and make sure you come up with a different spin on things.

> **Spotlight Swag:**
> *Is your HEAP not HEAP-ing?*
> *Check out Spotlight Swag at the back of this book for the Spotlight Starter Pack with ideas galore for press interviews!*

Chapter 3
Notice Me

 I'm not the messenger at all, I'm the message

– *Markus Zusak*

This chapter is a short one, but very important. As a producer on Smile Jamaica, I would get tons of pitches in email, by phone, and even in person. We've discussed why the competitive nature of the industry makes a good pitch important, but keep in mind, sometimes producers and reporters will search for their next story or interview by way of Google searches, Instagram deep dives, other media interviews, digging up business cards, and many other random, and sometimes quite strange ways. At the end of the day, we're looking, and if you'd like to be found, you need to have a presence that says '*notice me.*' I recognize that not everyone is social media savvy or tech-focused, but at the very minimum, we should be able to find you, get a grasp of what you're about, and contact you.

I'll be the first to admit, I'm not the best at social media or self promotion. I post pictures to my Instagram, but I've never had the discipline to post on schedule and maintain an organized timeline of my work and career. I'll tweet when I have nothing else to do, and I see Facebook perhaps once a month. What's worse for me is that social media is ever-evolving, and while I make an effort to keep up with the changes; I don't see myself committing to being a social star. So if you started this chapter thinking, 'here's where she tells me I need to be active on Instagram to get noticed,' don't you worry. What I will say is that you need some sort of presence. You may choose what that presence is, based on what you know you can commit to. However, you *must* commit to something. For me, it's a website. I spent time building my website and making sure it had strong and evergreen examples of my work. I made sure it had information to contact me and I established a blog that, even if I don't keep up with it, can be used for examples of my writing when necessary. I update my website bimonthly using whatever work I've already produced. People are able to send me messages and view my videos. If I'm ever applying for, or submitting a request for something special, I use a template that I made in the very beginning to create an individual page for whatever the cause is. It's the perfect amount of maintenance for me and I provide links to it on the social platforms I do use. So far, I've gotten many requests, collaborations, appearances and, yes, paid work through my website. Whatever works best and is easiest for you to maintain will do, but commit and make sure you keep up with it.

What We're Looking For

Where you have your presence is not as important as *what* is a part of your presence. For sure, the more pizazz you can add to your presence, the greater your chances will be of being noticed. But more isn't always merrier if it isn't done well and if you don't have the basics. I can't tell you how many times I think I've found someone spectacular only to realize their website or Facebook didn't have an email address or method of contact. Equally as many times I've gotten a reply to an Instagram or Twitter DM long after the fact and too late for me to work with them. When the press is looking for your presence, there are a couple of must haves - contact information being one of them. There are a few vital components most producers will be looking for, to *notice* you. These are the 4 C's:

Contact Information

As mentioned, this is number one. But take it a step further and have at least two methods of contact listed in an easy, obvious place. If I want you for an interview and you have a phone number and email listed, I'm going to email you immediately and follow up with a phone call. While social media has built in direct message features, many professionals prefer contacting you via email or phone. If needs be, create a separate email address and / or an alternate number (or Google Voice) for professional media inquiries and check that regularly. This also helps to keep any spam away from your personal affairs. If DM is your thing, consider adding a note indicating that you do indeed take professional inquiries through your direct messages. The more ways to reach you, the better your shot.

Content

I'm not a social media girl, remember? So fret not, I'm not asking you to sit around planning months of TikTok content or collect Instagram likes so you can get an interview. But the fact is your presence can't be empty.

Whoever you are and whatever you do needs to shine through. From a quick skim of whatever platform I'm looking at — whether it be your website, your Instagram or your Facebook page — I should have a solid idea of what you're about and what is special about you. That means you'll need to have some kind of content on your page, whether that be pictures, videos, text, testimonials or anything else. If you're a doctor for example, you may want to have a few videos of past interviews you've done giving your medical expertise. In the absence of that, photos of your degree along with one or two self-written accounts that show what you're an expert in. To illustrate this, I have 4 separate reels on my website - one for entertainment journalism, a producer reel, a spokesmodel reel and one for voice and podcasts.

Consistency

This is also very important, especially if you have multiple presences. If your website is that of a professional banker — suits, ties, client testimonials and money — but your public instagram is strippers and champagne, I'm going to think twice. Now I'm not being judgy. Be who you are. If there's anything you learn in this book, I want it to be that authenticity is key. But you must be consistent across any public presence you have. Otherwise, you'll get noticed for the wrong reasons. The thought process behind this notion is simply this: If I invite you as a guest on my show, how do I know which 'you' I'll get that day? Will I get the playboy or the professional? While I have a professional website; I also have an Instagram that chronicles my friends, fun and adventures. I'd been advised multiple times to make my Instagram private for fear of not being seen as a professional when I post pictures in swimsuits or sexy outfits. Despite that advice, I've branded myself as an entertainment journalist first with a flair for fun, excitement and electricity. My website is bright blue and gold (like the cover of this book) and matches the bright colors I wear on a daily basis. I also added a few story highlights of my reporting adventures so that you see that the same girl in front of the camera is the same one living this loud and authentic life. If your online presence lacks cohesion, it may be an issue of branding that you need to solve by going back to the drawing board. Inconsistency could also lead to issues with our next C.

Credibility

Although this ties in with authenticity, it is often a result of trying too hard. A lot of folks think they need a nice long resume or tons of samples and examples for the media to call on them. Yes, in some cases this is helpful, but it's quality and credibility that really counts. Producers and journalists want to know that you're reliable, that you are who you say you are, and that you can speak with expertise and share your story interestingly. If you start making up false press or pushing poorly constructed imagery of yourself, the person on the receiving end will likely figure it out quickly. Instead, stick to what is true and what you have solid proof of. Offer a reference or testimonials if you feel your presence is bare. If you want to create content, make sure that content is also credible and consistent. Even if you do manage to fool someone, it will unravel in the end and probably in a way detrimental to both you and the journalist. Remember my misadventures with Noor in the previous chapter? Yup.

Open Your Presence

If you've now started to think about what your presence should be, or you're thinking of upgrading what you currently have, I'd like to add a few items you may not have thought about. We're used to the obvious ones: a website, a social media page, etc. But getting noticed may also come by way of an in-person meeting, word-of-mouth or referral. As a producer, when I heard about someone or met someone directly, getting their information on the spot was always extremely helpful. Don't underestimate the power of having your information readily available in traditional and non traditional ways. Here are some ideas:

Business Card

My friends make fun of me for still having business cards, but you won't believe how many people call me months later and begin with 'I found your business card!' I also have a stack of cards and other material that I go through when I'm working on a segment or story. One thing that's important to note about your business card is that it shouldn't just have your name and contact info, it should ring a bell about who you are just in case one comes across it months later. Include your titles or what you do. Mine says 'Rae Williams - Entertainment Reporter | Producer | Writer.' In line with the consistency I've mentioned above, my cards are brightly colored and match the entire theme of my brand.

Press Kit

A press kit, or an electronic press kit (EPK), as they're sometimes referred to, is a few pages that contains key information about you, your brand or your business.

Whoever is looking can easily download it for perusal, or you can print it to distribute if needs be. My EPK includes my resume, links to my reels, photos, topics I can speak on, and a biography. It gives your presence a professional feel and makes it easy for whoever needs it to capture your info.

One Pager

This is essentially a press kit in truncated form with just enough information for the recipient to know who you are and what you're about. For my one pager, I skip the resume and most photos and include a shorter biography.

Brief

This one chops down the one pager even further into a paragraph or two that quickly describes who you are, your expertise and how to reach you. It is essentially a teaser for situations where you may not align totally with an outlet or journalist, but you want them to keep you in mind for the future. Mine is a postcard sized PDF with a few photos and limited text.

There is no limit to how creative you can be. My mother used to send out video introductions when applying for jobs and the feedback was fantastic. Be careful not to be too gimmicky and keep your credibility intact, but if you have time, make your presence solid so that you get noticed.

When Should You Reach Out to Press

There is a lot of debate about when you should reach out to the press, how many times you should follow up, and what you should include each time you reach out. The fact is this, 9 times out of 10 the person looking at your email or whatsapp or physical packet is…human. That means for as many producers and journalists that exist, there will be as many methods of when they check their email or take phone calls or look through pitches. The more you build a relationship with press people, the more you'll get to know how they operate. As a producer, I once had a guest who thoughtfully reached out periodically with other stories she thought I'd be interested in that had no connection to her. I appreciated this so much that when the ask was for her, I made an effort to accommodate her. It's less about when to reach out and more about building a genuine relationship. At the same time, use common sense and practicality when touching base. If you know a show tapes every Thursday at 2pm, then you know that Thursday at 1pm or even the day before is not likely to be a time when that producer or journalist is paying attention or taking phone calls. If you're trying to get press for an event or specific date; you may also want to consider sending with enough lead time for the producer to accommodate you; but not too early that they sweep it to the side and forget. From my experience, 3 weeks is a sweet spot.

Following Up

You've sent out your materials, it's been a few days and you haven't heard anything back, so you'd like to follow up. This isn't a problem, in fact, I encourage it. When you do follow up, however, don't simply send another blank message asking if they'd received your first message. Include a very brief overview or re-attach your brief or one-pager. Add a new detail. Don't send someone digging back for what you sent a week ago -- most won't even bother anyway. Sadly, most journalists I know will not reply if they're not interested. It's a matter of time rather than disrespect, honestly. I know a few gems who will politely tell you that they can't accommodate you, but just don't sit around expecting a reply if you haven't heard anything after one or two follow-ups.

There is much information floating around the web about specific times and dates to contact and follow up. Much of it is perfectly credible with research to back it up. It's worth taking a look and giving those times a shot if you align with it, but always remember that you're dealing with actual people with actual lives.

Reinvent Yourself

People ask me all the time what the key is to staying relevant in the media. While gimmicks and drama often do work, they're not the best strategies for long term relevance. Years ago, I posed the same question to Grammy winning Reggae artist Shaggy. His music career took off shortly after I was born, and there I was as a grown woman interviewing him about his career. I spoke to Shaggy again years after that encounter, this time alongside music legend Sting as they landed at a private airport in Jamaica. Again, Shaggy was still relevant with new music. Music that would go on to win him yet another Grammy. That wasn't the last I'd see of him. I interviewed Shaggy yet again - of course with new music - in 2020, and so I asked him again, 'What is the secret to longevity of career and staying relevant in the media?" His simple answer: Reinvent yourself. "I keep reinventing myself because nobody's going to be bored of me before I'm bored of me," he told me. "It's about making something that's so great that it fulfills me," he said. So make sure in all that you do, you're updating your presence, reinventing yourself and stepping outside yourself every so often. At my last interview with Shaggy, he offered me a bit of personal advice that I'll share with you. "You will never have growth unless you decide to be comfortable outside of your comfort zone," he said.

Part two

INTERVIEW ACADEMY

Chapter 4

Ten Press Preparation Tips

> *I believe luck is preparation meeting opportunity. If you hadn't been prepared when the opportunity came, you wouldn't have been lucky.*
>
> – Oprah

In my introduction, I mentioned getting lucky several times throughout my career. In the early stages, I was ready for whatever was thrown my way, but as I got further along, it became increasingly clear that the better prepared I was, the more fruitful my "luck". The good news is, by simply reading this book, you're getting ready for any interview opportunity that comes your way, and even taking it a step further by proactively securing your spots.

I wanted to dive in even further and specifically include my favorite ways to prepare for your upcoming interview, because I know better than anybody that bad preparation leads to bad press. Let me tell you a story.

I had an amazing side hustle in college designing and selling swimwear. Though it may seem random and far away from my film major, I actually grew up watching my grandmother design swimwear and was always in awe of her talent. Going to the University of Miami, two things were true: we were always at the beach, and the swimwear at the time was really expensive for your average college kid. Of course, I wanted to keep up with the girls who could drive their BMWs and Maseratis to the Luli Fama store and buy a $200 bikini without batting an eyelid. But the truth was I couldn't bring myself to spend my extra money from my server job that way. So I thought, why not make my own? A few visits to the fabric stores downtown, a few experiments with cutting and sewing, and a few helpful google searches later, I had my first bikini made. Everybody wanted to know where I got it. When I told them I'd made it myself, everybody wanted me to make them one. That's how my swimwear line WildFreeForever was born. I made swimsuits for the pageants on campus. I did custom orders and before I knew it, I had set up both a website and an Etsy store, had professional photos taken of my swimwear and it was *a thing*. When I was invited to participate in Caribbean Fashion Week in Jamaica shortly after graduation, I was extremely thrilled. I did interviews with newspapers and TV shows and before I knew it my side hustle became an actual business. Back then, even though I was a newly-minted film school graduate and had taken multiple courses in media, I was so excited for all the opportunities coming my way, I never once stopped to think about how I was presenting myself to the press. My products were speaking for themselves, so I didn't even think to prepare. One day I got a call from a producer at Television Jamaica. I'd been out of touch with the station for several years after my two summer runs as a producer, and now this time, I was being invited to be a *guest* on the morning show. *What?!* I was so excited. *Of course!* She already had an idea for the segment, as producers sometimes will. She said my swimwear reminded her of a few retro styles and she wanted me to talk about swimwear over the years. She gave me homework: send in graphics to go with my segment and bring in a few examples of my own swimwear. I immediately called models (*ok, I called a few close friends and begged them to appear on national television in my pieces, promising they could wear more conservative designs*), and I got to work deciding what I was going to talk about and planning where I would go with my segment. You may be saying at this point, "*ok, Rae, so you prepared*". Except I kind of didn't. I decided I was going to give a swimsuit to the show's host. It was a perfect 'marketing plot'. Who didn't like getting gifts and what better way to get my swimsuit worn by someone popular? That morning, my segment went exactly as planned -- until the end. As we wrapped, live on-air I gifted the host her bathing suit in my signature leather-look drawstring bag with neon-pink drawstring. Her reaction was just what I wanted. Happy and elated, she opened it immediately and pulled out the pink, purple swirled, snake-skin teeny bikini. All at once, her face of excitement, turned to one of embarrassment and shock, and she jammed the bikini back into the bag and wrapped the segment in 25 seconds flat. I didn't understand. Maybe she didn't like it? Maybe it was the wrong size? It wasn't until that afternoon when I was waiting for jerked chicken at a restaurant window that I discovered the real reason for her reaction. " I saw you on TV today!" the lady on the other side of the window said. "Pretty swimsuits, but why did you give the host one that was so small. You didn't know she's a Christian?" Nope. I actually didn't know. I had planned my segment, and I had planned for me, but I hadn't researched the host. If I had, I would have known about her very public transition into a far more conservative, Christian lifestyle. I would have known to present her with a more modest style that embraced that. Not an itsy bitsy flashy bikini that she wouldn't dare wear. Whoops. Big whoops. People would remember two things: Yes, my swimsuits were dope. But also, I'd given their beloved conservative host the wildest bikini in my collection. Two seconds of googling would have saved me. So here's where I give you the cliche "fail to plan and you plan to fail," but also where I specifically tell you *how* to plan. My first press preparation tip, of course, is *do your research*.

1. Research

I can't lead with this tip without giving you another example. This time from the perspective of a reporter. I was assigned to cover America's Got Talent: Champions. The line up: AGT winners from years gone by, the muse Heidi Klum - I respected her endlessly from my design days, Simon Cowell, Howie Mandell, Terry Crews, Alishia Dixon. *Wow*. This was going to be a big one. So naturally, I meticulously planned my outfit, reviewed past seasons of the show, looked up driving directions ahead of time, etc. What did I not do? Sit down and meticulously research the people I'd be interviewing. Now let me start by saying, Red Carpets are really tricky to prepare for. Sometimes you get a list of people ahead of time. Most times, the majority of those people don't show up. Many times, they do show up but choose not to interview with you. It's all a novice game of chess and sometimes you're just a pawn. That day however, I was the queen. Every single person showed up, and all accepted interviews with me. Heidi Klum and Simon Cowell BOTH told me they liked my dress. Then Howie Mandell came up. As I do at the beginning of every interview, I stuck out my hand for a handshake while introducing myself. "Hi I'm Rae from the Buzz," I said, waiting for him to take my hand. But he didn't. Instead he looked at me like a wild animal. There was an awkward 7-second pause, where neither of us did or said anything. He slowly raised his hand into a fist, and said "We can do this," raising his hand into fist bump formation. "Ok," I said confused. His eyes never left me as I fist bumped him back. The rest of the interview was extremely strange. Howie kept backing away from me as I spoke, I kept trying to move closer and he was very suspicious of every movement I made while I struggled to read his behavior and direct the interview.

When it finally ended, my producer took off his headphones and let out a bellowing laugh. "What?" I asked him. Then he laughed even more until tears came to his eyes. When he finally got to speaking, he looked at my confused face and said. "That's my bad, I should have told you Howie is a huge germaphobe. The second you tried to shake his hand, he didn't trust you. My bad, I should have told you. But that whole interview was hilarious. It was gold. My bad." I was *bewildered*. But the truth is, it wasn't my producer's 'bad'. It was mine. I should have done my research. I should have sat down and studied past interviews with all the judges and researched beyond just the recent events of the show. Even if I didn't get an interview with Howie that day, the knowledge would have come in handy somewhere down the line. Research anything you can think of: your interviewer, the outlet, the audience, the station's viewership numbers. If your mind touches on it, it's worth doing some research on. Each tip that follows should trigger additional thoughts of things you can research.

2. Ask Questions

I'm sure you've heard at some point in your life "there's no such thing as a stupid question." That is not my belief. There are plenty of dumb questions. As a reporter, the most unproductive thing you can do is ask someone whose son just died in a fire 'how are you feeling,' *Shocked. Sad. Obviously.* But this is your one time to ask all your questions of your producer so you *don't* end up looking dumb during your interview. Keeping in mind that the producer's time is probably limited, take your chance to ask anything you feel will help you enhance your interview. Here are some good ones to start with:

1. *The date, time and location of the interview.* Sounds like a no-brainer, but please ask this and repeat it at some point to confirm. Missing an interview, or being late is the quickest way to get struck off a producer's list. You have to know so you can go!

2. *The name of your interviewer.* You want to know this ahead of time to research them, of course, so you have a face and information to match the name.

3. *What angle do you want to approach this with?* This could help to inform how you prepare for your segment

4. *What is the format?* As we learned from the chapters before, each format has its own demands, so you need to know what you're dealing with.

5. *When will this run?* Have an event happening tomorrow? Great! But since you asked this question, you'll know this interview will air afterwards and you won't waste time talking about it.

6. *Can I share this?* I've done segments that are 'embargoed' until a certain date. Be sure to ask the producer if and when you can share so you don't let the cat out of the bag before its time.

3. Decide your story and your examples

If you pitched this interview to the outlet following the advice from previous chapters, you should have a solid foundation for what story you want to tell and examples to use. If you were approached for this interview, part of your prep should be to sit down and decide what your content will be for this interview. Remember, much like when you're pitching, your interview content should have a HEAP - Humble brag, Examples, Action and Personal touch.

4. Prepare for the pre-interview

The majority of times, you will have a pre-interview before the interview itself. This may not be something formal, and it may actually occur at the time you're approached or shortly after you pitched, or even when you're asking questions. At times the pre-interview may take the format of written questions they want you to send in ahead of time. Your pre-interview may be conducted by a producer or even 15 minutes before your actual interview by the hosts. Think of it as the conversation before the conversation. You still want to put your best foot forward in the pre-interview to best strengthen your relationship with the outlet. When in a pre-interview be sure to:

- *Bring your energy.* You want whoever it is to get excited about having you interviewed. It may even lead to a few perks, like your segment being promoted or an excellent time slot on the slow.

- *Be accurate.* Make sure your statistics are real and ready, disclose whatever disclosures you may have. Keep in mind the pre-interviewer may be taking notes for use in the interview and/or for graphics, host sheet or anything else for the actual interview.

- *Give soundbites.* Consider this practice for your real interview, and as mentioned above, the more impressive you are, the better chance you have of perks.
- *Take notes.* The pre-interview may give you clues as to what the producer is hoping to achieve, even beyond the answer they give you when you ask questions.
- *Offer help.* Would they like you to send over a one-pager? Do they need you to spell your name correctly? See where you can offer a bit of help, but don't push it if the person says no.

5. Have a statistic in your toolkit

As I'll explain a little later, a statistic can be your savior. It's always good to outline and memorize 3 or 4 statistics that you have on hand for your interview. These don't have to be numbers, they can be a bit more abstract like, "about half of the people we tried this method on expressed shock at their result." Just make sure the statistics are ballpark accurate, and don't be afraid to add some personality to it. Instead of '950 people die every year from the diseases our company's drug helps to save', try '500 mothers will leave children behind this year, and we can do something about that'.

6. **Practice in the mirror. Practice on a friend.**

I don't care how far my career gets or who I encounter, I will always be the biggest advocate of practice. It may feel awkward at first, but practice your talking points in the mirror, out loud to yourself. When you've done that, practice with a friend or family member. Record yourself with your phone and take note of improvements you'd like to make. You do not want the first time the words come out of your mouth to be when the camera is rolling or the voice recorder is on. After the mirror, I have a few go-tos when I practice. If I'm doing an audition, I'll face-time my mom and deliver my lines or script or ad-lib to her. I'll take a mental note of when or if she laughs. She'll tell me where I went too fast and she got lost. I can see her facial expressions and know whether or not she's with me. If I'm doing an interview, I'll call my dad and say, for example, "What questions do you have for Dionne Warwick?" After all, I'm conducting the interview on behalf of the public, so if there's something he's curious about that I didn't think about, I'll add it to my list. I'll then practice the questions on my list and sometimes I'll get feedback like 'Don't ask her that! That's been beaten to death.' If I'm presenting or speaking, I'll give a highlight presentation to my godmother, who will always add insight or tell me where she would love to hear me dig in further. The final determination is always mine, but their feedback and advice is always invaluable.

7. Arrive Early

Please take this valuable tip from the latest person on earth. Seriously, I'm always late. And I *know* I'm always late. And *my friends* know I'm always late. But you know who doesn't care that *late* is actually a personality trait of mine? The people I'm interviewing. The people I'm being interviewed by. The people who are signing my checks. So this late girl, makes provisions for her lateness by planning far ahead and giving an allowance for the inevitables like traffic, parking, walking to the location, spilling coffee on my outfit before I head out the door or an extra long goodbye session with my dogs. You don't want to be on time either. On time means being rushed into to make up and potentially shoved on a set before you have time to catch your breath. It could mean you have to run up 5,000 steps to get to the reporter's office on the other side of the property, making you late even though technically you were on time. There is no bigger relief for a producer than realizing their next interviewee is already present and prepped to go. My rule? Plan to arrive 15 minutes early, check in and sit quietly while everyone does their job. If your call-time has arrived and no one has come to get you, politely check in again.

8. Promote it

In a world dominated by social media, an upcoming interview, especially if it's live, is something that you'll want to share when you have permission to do so. Drop a teaser if you can. Engage people. Get people to tune in. Get people excited for your segment. Your audience is now the outlet's audience and they will appreciate the extra eyes.

9. Prepare your outfit

If this question just made you think 'Oh crap. What do I even wear to an interview?`` Don't worry! I've got you covered in the next chapter. But once you know the guidelines of what to wear, prepare your outfit ahead of time and prepare a backup to bring with you (because, coffee spills). The last thing you want to be doing an hour before your interview, is changing outfits 19 times.

10. Leave your devices (or at least really, truly silence them)

I really should write a list called 'Ways to Piss Off a Producer" and this would definitely be on there (number one would be being late!). Unless you're the Queen of England, your device going off during our interview is not okay - and even the Queen would never! Seriously. Turn off your telephone, iPad, Smart Watch or anything else that may make a noise and disrupt our interview. If you need to have your phone in the interview to take selfies after, make sure it's completely silenced. Not on vibrate (we can hear that). *Silenced.*

What if the interview is a surprise?

Of course, there are times when you don't have the opportunity to go through the motions above and truly prepare for an interview. By the time you finish this book, you should have a general preparation and tools in place and enough basic knowledge to always be ready, but what do you do if the interview is really, truly a surprise? There are a couple instances where this could happen. Maybe the reporter is on a deadline, or maybe they're ambushing you on purpose. A lot of media trainers will advise you not to do the interview, to instead say you'll call them back and take time to prepare, but I say shoot your shot. This might be it. Of course, I'll give you some guidelines for winging it if you haven't had time to prep for an interview:

1. *Make sure you understand the outlet.* Surprise or not, ask what the outlet is so you can mentally tailor your message. Is it a conservative radio station asking you to give an audio interview? Is it a teen magazine asking you to comment on Kylie Jenner's latest makeup line? Asking the simple question will equip you just enough to narrow your message.
2. *Give a short, concise statement.* Don't try to drag on. This is where mastering your message comes in handy, but beware of giving a lengthy interview with lots of misplaced details if you haven't prepared.
3. *Offer to follow up.* Especially if you feel like you could have done better, offer to send further information by email or to come in studio for a more in depth chat. This gives you a great opportunity to do some homework, build a relationship, and secure a further interview. They may not take you up on the offer, but you never know.

After the interview

Although this chapter is about preparation, I wanted to add in a few things to do after your interview is over. You want to leave everyone with whom you come in contact with a great memory of you, and it's easy to do.

1. *Say thank you* - This really should be a no brainer, but you wouldn't believe how many times I bent over backwards as a producer to accomodate someone who didn't even say thank you. Say it in person. Send a quick email. It doesn't have to be anything fancy, just say thank you.

2. *Follow up and see when it will air* - If you didn't get an answer to this before, it's a great question to ask after.

3. *Don't try to control the editing / article* - File this one under my imaginary list of "Ways to Piss Off a Producer". There's nothing more aggravating than an interviewee trying to control the end product of a piece or interview. There's a reason the producer is the producer. There's a reason we have an editor, a host, an audio technician and a camera person. You want a shot cut out because you look fat. Too bad! We don't have the time nor energy to massage each piece we do into something that satisfies the

interviewee. If there's a factual error or inaccuracy, by all means, please call it out, but otherwise, leave your vanity at home.

4. *Share* - Share your interview and direct people to how they can access it. If permitted, post it on your social channels and try to get a copy for your files.

Spotlight Swag:
Check out quick reference versions of the checklists above in the last chapter of this book!

Chapter 5
Let's Get Physical

> *When you become the image of your own imagination - it's the most powerful thing you could ever do*
>
> – RuPaul

Welcome to one of my favorite chapters of the book, and also, the chapter I almost didn't write. Why? Because this chapter was originally meant to focus on dressing for an interview, especially a video interview, and I felt that I was in no position to comment on anyone's appearance or personal style. As I found myself on more and more Red Carpets and attending more and more Hollywood events, rubbing shoulders with some of the industry's most styled and most stylish, my sense of style became heightened and sharpened, and I realized that your appearance, especially when talking to the media, is *never* just what you're wearing. It's your entire physical presence - your clothing, your confidence, your stride, your swag - the image you project. While your outfit is important, so much more contributes to your appearance. Now, I'll admit, I don't consider myself to be the most fashionable, and I still get lazy or play it safe when it comes to what I wear; there are a few physical things I never compromise on and they're all components of my body language. I call them SEERS.

> **S** - Stand (or sit) tall
>
> **E** - Energy
>
> **E** - Eyes
>
> **R** - React
>
> **S** - Speak up

These may seem pretty straight forward, but I'm willing to bet that at any given time, you aren't doing one of these. Not only are these components of your body language super valuable in interviews, they're actually great just for everyday interactions. I'll never forget on my 30th birthday, getting into a super-exclusive celeb lounge in West Hollywood. One of those types of places you can't take pictures in because of the high profile clientele. You need a reservation way ahead of time and a friend of mine announced 30 minutes prior to heading out that that's where we were going. When we got to the door she walked straight up and after a 3 minute conversation she waved us over and we filed inside. "Did you know somebody at the door?" I asked her. "Nope," she replied. I just convinced them that we are supposed to be here. When I thought about it, she really used SEERS to get us through the door. She walked tall like she was a celebrity herself. Her energy reflected the vibe of the place we were getting into - upscale, refined, not too loud, but firm. She made direct eye contact when she was speaking, she was clear and confident, projecting instead of mumbling. If my friend could use that to unlock the doors of exclusivity, imagine what improving your body language can do for your interview, whether print, audio, video or social. Let's break down these components a bit:

Stand (or sit) tall

Whether or not your interviewer can see you, standing or sitting with your back straight and shoulders back, automatically adds to your confidence. It's been proven time and again that this great posture equals great power and signals to your brain that the most confident part of you is in charge.

Energy

When I say energy here, I don't mean be your loudest or shout at your interviewer. What I mean here is ensure that your energy matches your message and the medium. If you're a Yoga practitioner, you want your nature to be one that's calming and inspirational, but if you're a clown, you'll vibrate energy as high as you possibly can. There's a fine line between matching your energy and making sure you actually *have* energy. Even if you're extending a calm nature, you never want to come across impassive and boring. Before your interview, do a few exercises to get your blood pumping. Whether I'm the interviewer, or the interviewee, I always do a little swaying dance as I'm preparing. You know that dance little kids do when they get candy? Yup, that's my dance. To this day, crewmembers mock it and it's become somewhat of a signature. It's my way of waking up my body.

Eye Contact

I know I sound like your grandmother when I say this, but look at people when you're speaking to them unless directed otherwise - and there will be times you're directed otherwise. Think of most interviews as a conversation and look at your interviewer. Even if you're being interviewed for a print piece, relate with eye contact. It's been said that you need to make eye contact with someone 60% - 70% of the time of your conversation to make an emotional connection. You don't have to stare, but since it's also been reported that most adults only make eye contact 30% - 60% of the time, you may want to practice this. If you're instructed to look at the camera, then do just that. Practice keeping your eyes steady by recording yourself on your phone. Avoid darting your eyes or looking back at the interviewer for approval. You don't need to see your business partner and you really, really don't need to look at your phone(!). If you're asked to look in a direction that's away from your interviewer and the camera, find a focal point within your direct eye line and keep your eyes there.

React

I once worked for a company where the CEO told us that when speaking to our clients, we shouldn't say "mhm" or nod our heads or acknowledge them in any way. He claimed it would make them feel rushed or like we were just trying to get them to get it all out. I tried it out a few times on the phone, via video and in person and the response was the same every time - "are you there?" "does that make sense?" "hello?". Without a reaction of some kind, they thought I wasn't even paying attention. No matter what the medium is, react genuinely and appropriately to your interviewer. The only thing that doesn't deserve a reaction is the distractive stimuli around you. Whether it's a resounding YES! Or a hand over your heart to agree with a statement you really feel, the name of the game here is authenticity.

Speak Up

If you're bringing the energy you need into your interview, this should come a little more naturally, but it's important to speak up. An interview is not a place to whisper, mumble or otherwise communicate ineffectively. Even if you're writing in, the confidence in your voice should come across. Again, just like with projecting energy, I'm not saying be loud if you're not a naturally loud person. Confidence can coexist with authenticity. Practice clarity and voice projection whenever you speak.

When assessing your body language, it's also important to realize that every single one of us has ticks and natural reactions to stress and surprises. I call these anxiety points. For some, it's cracking their knuckles, for others it's a furrowed brow. For me, it's my entire face. Yes, my *entire* face. Resting b*tch face is not something that happens to me, because my face has a reaction to everything and its own special style of concentration. In fact, when I'm concentrating, I tend to look confused. I didn't realize it until I started hosting *Entertainment Report*, an entertainment magazine television program. On our very first shoot, my producer, a widely known and acclaimed entertainment journalism veteran, shouted as I was reading from the teleprompter "you look confused! Do you understand what you're reading?" It was confusing to me, because I *wasn't* confused. I understood what I was reading. He handed me the script after the shoot and said, "take this home and practice in the mirror. Watch the show after, you'll see what I mean." I did both and boy was I surprised. In the moments I thought I was just simply processing information internally, it was right there in the mirror and on the TV screen - right on my face. My thinking face looks confused and in that setting the confusion comes across as a lack of confidence. "Oh, no, no, no," I thought to myself. I had to fix that ASAP, and the only way to do that was practice.

If you've done a recorded interview before, look back at it and notice if there are things you do when nervous, or surprised by a question, or thinking really hard. If you don't have anything to look at, practice answering questions in the mirror and see if anything comes up. The habit you have probably isn't just relegated to interviews, so pick a day to pay special attention to your body language and make any observations. The people around you will most likely pick up on any special behaviors too, so feel free to ask a friend.

> **Spotlight Swag:**
> *Need some interview questions to ask yourself in the mirror? Find some in chapter 10!*

Time to Get Dressed

One of the questions I got frequently as a producer was 'what do I wear to this interview?' Now again, while I'm not here to coach you on personal style, there are a few guidelines that you may want to employ, especially for on-camera interviews. If you're thinking, "but I really do need some personal style pointers," to help you get your style on, I actually turned to a few expert friends for advice. First, a few basics for video:

- *No Green* - Ask ahead of time if the interview is taking place in front of a green screen, and if you're not sure, stay away from green or greeny-blues. If you're going to be in front of a green screen, don't wear any shade of green. They'll filter the screen in post production and turn it into a lovely background. If you're wearing green, you'll become a part of the background too. The only fix for this if you show up in green attire is to change your clothes. I'll tell you a secret: Almost every studio has an extra large, musty jacket that's been there for a decade that they use for when people show up in green. You don't want to have to put that on. Trust me.

- *Avoid Very Shiny Clothing* - Even people that know about the green rule mess up on this one. Shiny clothing can reflect the green screen, creating the same effect as noted above. Even if there is no green screen, a super shiny shirt can reflect an image of the camera or behind the scenes and come across as disruptive. Here's a helpful hint: Transparent articles don't work on a green screen either. I may or may not have had to stalk the newsroom to find a fellow reporter with size 11 feet to replace the transparent heels I brought to film in one day. So I know this one!

- *Avoid Spots, Dots and Stripes* - Spots, dots and stripes can come across as confusing. Stripes especially can create something called the moiré pattern, where the pattern clashes and competes with others around it, distorting it. Though you can get away with some big patterns, the smaller it is, the bigger the risk. Solid-colored clothing is best. However, let me say this: If your outfit is a part of your brand or image, then by all means come in your red stripes and spotted Gucci shoes - I'm here for you! But even within the parameters of your personality, be aware of the ground rules on a set. In a little while, we'll go deeper into how you can translate your personal style for camera while following the rules.

- *Consider where the mic will go* - For a lot of video interviews, you'll have to be mic'd up. The mic, called a lavalier, is a small clip-on device usually with a long power cord. Every good producer, photographer or sound engineer will want to ensure that this cord is hidden, meaning they'll want you to conceal it under your clothing. Once that cord is concealed, they'll need to clip the mic somewhere. If you're wearing a high neckline or a unitard or something very complicated, it will be difficult to find a place to hide the cord or clip the mic. While the majority of times this is a figureoutable problem; the production you're a part of may not have time to dedicate to this. After years in the business, I'm still super guilty of this and have learned to identify the long sigh that signals the thought, "how are we going to mic her?" Don't be like me friends! Unless, your outfit is a part of your personality brand or your segment, keep these considerations in mind.

- *Don't Wear Full White or Black* - "But Rae, didn't you just say wear solids?" I did. But full white can be visually overwhelming and hard to balance on the camera. Especially if you have darker skin, the cameraperson will have to do some extra tweaks to make sure that your clothing isn't washed out while maintaining the brilliance of your brown skin! Guess what? The same stands for all black too. I can hear you complaining that "black is slimming," but black is also light absorbing, again adding complications for your camera person as they try to neutralize the contrast.

- *Dress for the occasion* - Would you wear a ballgown to a baseball game? Nope! So don't appear for an interview on a business show in torn jeans and an old tshirt. From the questions you ask during your prep, you should know the type of show and the audience.

- *Make Sure You're Comfortable* - The worst thing is to spend the entirety of your interview tugging at your outfit. *Thinking* about tugging at your outfit because you're worried something is off is just as distracting. Make sure you're comfortable in whatever you choose.

- *Bring a Change of Clothes and a Towel* - It's always safe to have a just-in-case outfit as well as a hand towel to blot if you need to. I sweat instantly under any kind of bright lights - even the ones in a make-up room, so I always have a change of outfit just in case. This also helps if for some reason the producer has an issue with your outfit or if your choice of attire is somehow clashing with the set or host. It's not a bad idea to bring a comb or brush for quick touch-ups either!

- *Basic Makeup* - Not every production has a make-up artist on hand, but for those that do, they'll be happy to fix you up for your segment. But there's something very important to understand about TV make-up: It's not necessarily the kind that you wear in everyday life. Depending on your production, the make-up artists on hand may give you a very dramatic look or a very quick, basic look. Don't worry if you don't look 'normal', it will translate on camera. I've seen so many people walk in with demands for the make-up artists that were impossible because of either time constraints or practicality. If you need something very specific, try to clear it with the producer ahead of time. If you have a preference of makeup or tools, bring it with you and ask politely if your stuff can be used. I've also seen a lot of men protest makeup, but what you need to understand is that, for men, the makeup is to prevent shine rather than make you look "pretty". You'll regret requesting no makeup when all you can look at is your shiny forehead, or shiny bald head during the interview.

- *Camera Test Your Outfit* - Grab a friend and a phone and give it a spin. Answer some mock questions or practice your stats. Are you sweating like crazy after motioning? Did you get up to demonstrate and almost break your ankle in your five inch heels? Does that tie actually look Oscar the Grouch green on camera? Do your lady parts peek out when you're seated? Men - are your twig and berries a bit too prominent in those pants? Good thing you tested! Now you can make the necessary changes.

It took me quite a while to find my personal spotlight style. However, I can attest to the fact that once you do find it, it makes your interviews that much stronger. So how do you find it? As I mentioned, I'm by no means a stylist or style expert. I am, however, someone who knows someone who is. I turned to Anya Ayoung-Chee. You may recognize Anya from being the winner of season 9 of Bravo's Emmy-winning competition series **Project Runway,** but her credits definitely don't stop there. She was also Miss Trinidad and Tobago Universe 2008, and is a television host, philanthropist, and of course, an exceptionally talented stylist and designer. From carnival costumes, to lingerie, to resort-wear, Anya has seen and styled it all. I had so many questions to ask her, but I had to start with what I struggled with most when first coming into my own. *What the hell is personal style? Is that different from fashion? Am I trendy? Should I be trendy?*

Anya's first piece of advice is don't get too caught up in 'fashion', which she simply describes as what's trending. "Fashion can sometimes lead you astray from your personal style because you can get caught up in what's popular versus what you actually like," Anya says. "I would put what you actually like in the category of personal style." It's not that simple, though. "Sometimes that takes a little bit of digging deep into yourself to say that you actually resonate with this silhouette, or you recognize from advice from designers or from your friends that these silhouettes fit your body," she says.

"I think personal style is best when it's a combination of what you actually like and aesthetics that you're drawn to, [and then] married to what suits your body, what suits your skin color and what suits your everything. It does take a bit of courage, research and work to keep trying new things and make sure that you get to the point where you do have a personal style. And, of course, your personal style evolves. Your personal style at 25 is likely not the same as when you're 35." In other words, don't sweat it if in your first on-camera interview, you look like a penguin (yes, this happened to me). Watch and learn from yourself and be willing to branch out.

The next thing I wondered about was your style's role in your branding, especially after everything we've discussed so far. If you're a doctor, do you show up to your interview in scrubs, or can you dress up? Do you always need to be in a company shirt, or can you don a suit? There's no right or wrong way to do this. It's a personal choice that goes beyond your clothing and into your authenticity. Anya says from the time she was able to make the choice about what she wore, she did. She says the role of style in your personal brand is *everything*. "It's the first thing someone sees when they meet you, and it's everything from the way you do your hair to the way you do your nails. Not just clothes. Fashion is a combination of all of these choices that you make for your body and aesthetic presence." So maybe you're a dermatologist promoting your skincare line and you feel your sleek white coat gives off an air of professionalism and luxury, you can inject your style in there in your choice of shoes, or eyewear, or an eye-catching brooch.

Anya also makes it clear that you do not have to be outrageous. "It can be understated," she says. "Nobody's saying that's your personal style, and therefore, your brand has to be loud and distinct. If your personal style is more minimal, that is also a brand. Ideally everything should have the same consistency, tone and recognizable energy around it, and that all comes from being authentic."

So where do you start? Especially in the early stages, you may not have the capacity to spend a great amount of money on clothes. Anya's answer to this: separates and statement pieces. "It's very easy to have one dress, one jumpsuit, one whatever and not have to match anything else because it's just one piece," Anya adds. "But when you have separates you can mix and match a lot more. You can have a great statement pair of pants. A great statement white shirt. Certain things are classic. Then you can combine them in ways that stretch the use for forever and ever." This advice bodes well for all genders.

Once your interview frequency starts picking up, you may be concerned about repeating outfits. Don't! If you find you're really heavy on repetition, Anya says own that. But there are also creative ways of getting around this. She recalls the millions of appointments and interviews she had after winning Project Runway. "It was impossible to keep up," she said. But also not one to throw things away or never wear them again, she found solutions. Firstly, she says, if you're going to wear the same thing twice, you should either make a statement about it or don't make it a big thing at all. "The Duchess of Cambridge blatantly wears things multiple times and it's spoken about in a very positive way," Anya points out. "For somebody like that to be so brave says a lot. If people question you about it, you can have a stance. For example: "I don't want to contribute to the massive amount of waste that fast fashion has on the environment, and so I'm okay with wearing things over and over again."

A bit earlier, I mentioned translating your personal style within the parameters of the on-camera rules. Anya is an expert here, too. She says firstly, keep in mind the rules are there to make you look good. "There are definitely times when you don't realize how things are coming across," she says. "I always look at it as a puzzle. Follow the rules creatively." Prints are a prime example. If these are absolutely your style, Anya advises to wear them, but wear them smartly. She recommends avoiding small prints because of the moiré effect mentioned before. "It looks like static," she says. "Do bold prints, or really graphic prints. Not too fine or detailed because it gets lost." She continues on how to maximize your look, even as a minimalist. "Even if you're a minimal person, avoid things that are too simple because then you just wash out. If you're of minimal taste, things like color blocking, work really well on camera. Even if you're going for a monochromatic look, choose a slightly more bold color than you want. If you like rosé, wear coral. Remember: Camera lights wash you out."

Also, she suggests considering the shot, or angles if you're doing photos. "If you have a situation where you're wearing off-the-shoulder or sleeveless and it's a bunch of close shots, all of a sudden you look naked and that's not what you want," Anya says. "Don't be afraid to ask about the shot or color of the background or 'are there any colors that I'm going to clash or blend with on set?' I'll do a little research if it's a show that I know of to find out what their logo looks like and if there are going to be any colors that I'm competing with. Of course you want to stand out, but you want to do it in a way that makes sense." If you feel the rules are restrictive, Anya asserts, "Let's say they tell you - no short skirts, no shoulders, no black, no white. Okay - that leaves me with all of these other options still. Sometimes you can get caught up with what you can't do, when the fun of it is figuring out what you can do."

Finally, if you do get to a point where you are being styled or can afford to hire a stylist, you can still make sure your authenticity shines through. Try Anya's tips for getting a stylist or designer for yourself:

1. Go with one single designer who you trust and vibe with
2. Get a range of things that suit different arrangements

3. Come with a Pinterest board or some other collage of what you like and what resonates with you.

"99% of stylists are visual people," Anya says. "A graphic representation will open up the conversation to saying 'how do we get there for you?'" She adds that, "somebody who gets offended if you offer your own inspiration is not the right person to begin with. A good stylist will be honest with you if the job is not for them."

When it comes to appointed stylists, it may be tricky if you feel like their vision is not in line with yours. "That's a tough one, only because it does somewhat depend on your positioning in relation to the stylist," Anya says, recognizing that this is a situation newcomers often end up in. "Some people are very well respected, but you should always have autonomy. Revert to that same method as if you were approaching a stylist of your choosing and say, 'I've put together this board of images that make me feel like this is what expresses me' or 'here are a few clothing lines that I really love'. If they are a professional, they'll want you to feel as great as you should feel. If you don't say anything, It's like going to have your car fixed and then you don't want the mechanic to feel bad about the fact that your car still doesn't work. That's the person's job," Anya emphasizes.

However you choose to approach it, remember the baseline rules and remember that authenticity goes above all else.

Spotlight Swag:
Anticipating a lot of interviews and ready to build a media wardrobe? Check out the last chapter for my Spotlight Style Basics list to get you started!

Chapter 6
Breaking Bad (Habits)

> *The truth is, you don't break a bad habit, you replace it with a good one*
>
> – Dennis Waitley

How do I stop saying 'um'? My eyes look crazy when I look at the camera. I feel like I'm rambling. We've all seen them, and we all have them: Habits that likely have no effect on our day-to-day lives, but come across terribly in media interviews. We tend to call these habits 'bad' ones. No one is born perfectly media trained, so before we discuss some of these habits, it's important to discuss that the key here is not necessarily stopping these habits, but replacing them with better ones or improving upon the habit we have. We'll discuss the 10 most common habits shortly, but first, I want to confess mine. *Of course.*

Of. Course. That's it. That's the habit. "*Of course*" is my favorite phrase in any interview. I'm not sure why or when it happened, but I tend to start sentences with, "of course." Especially when I'm in high-pressure interviews such as on a Red Carpet with a guest I didn't expect; I use those two little words, followed by a general intro sentence, as fillers while my brain formulates the next question. "Of course, we're here at ___ event for ___ cause and we have the wonderful ___ with us!" "Of course, we're speaking to the best-dressed man in Hollywood." "Of course, you know what I have to ask you first." I'll watch interviews I did and think, "OF COURSE you said of course." But the thing is, sometimes I *need* that beat. Most of us need that beat to gather our thoughts whether we're brand new to this or we've been doing it for 20 years. So how do you take that quick moment you need to think while not seeming untrained? How do you keep eye contact when you need to glance at a timer to see how long you have left on air? How do you respectfully address someone without messing up their pronouns or preferred title? Again, the key here isn't so much completely eradicating these habits from our mental space altogether; as it is making them more productive. While there is no magic fix to any of these habits, once you've identified your habit, you can find a way to flip it. And, of course, the key here is practice. Let's walk through some common concerns:

Habit:
Problematic Fillers and Verbal Tics
(Ums, ahhs, likes, and ahms)
The Solution:
Inhale and Exhale

Fillers and verbal tics are by far the most common habit and the one that people are most self-conscious of. In fact, a lot of people tell me the main reason they're terrified to do interviews is that they are afraid they'll sound stupid because they 'um' and 'ahh' so much. Luckily, this habit can be easily defeated with a little patience and practice.

First, you'll want to identify when it is that you use a filler or your tic shows the most. Is it when you're using numbers? Is it when you're explaining concepts? When you have to introduce yourself? When someone asks a question? This will take a lot of awareness and patience, but it's helpful in the long run for figuring out exactly when you need to take action. You don't have to wait for an actual media interview to figure this out either. Chances are, whatever your filler or tic is, it's something you use in everyday life too. So listen to yourself on phone calls, in meetings, when having intense discussions. Don't be afraid to record yourself and listen back too (with the other parties' consent, of course). Fillers and tics are commonly the results of one of a few things:

1. You're talking too fast
2. You're rambling
3. You're unprepared

So before we even replace this habit with anything else, let's first make sure we're talking at a generous, yet productive pace - that is *just* fast enough to portray energy, but slow enough so that every word can be understood, ideas can land properly on your audience, and most of all, so you don't trip yourself up. We'll also want to make sure we're not rambling on and on. We'll talk about exactly how to correct that next, as well as how to prepare even when you don't have much time.

Whatever the reason, linguists say tics and verbal fillers, especially 'um', usually indicate the need to think something through or recall information. In other words, you need a pause. That pause allows us to get back on track, and choose our next words or ideas. So if you need a pause, why not pause *effectively*.

If you're tackling a difficult subject matter, or you know you're prone to 'ums' and 'ahs', a great way to take your pause effectively, is replacing your fillers with a great big inhale and exhale. Any public speaking class you'll take will teach you the importance of breathing, so this trick builds on that method. This is not just any old inhale-for-oxygen breath, though. This inhale will be deep, and the exhale should expend energy and passion. Once you master that, you can take it a step further by using your hand motions to reflect the action of your grand inhale and exhale. Not only do you give yourself a beat to catch up, but you also feed yourself a little extra oxygen and convey energy and emotion to your audience.

Habit:
Rambling (and also, mansplaining and sounding preachy)
Solution:
Prepare Three Parts

Another habit that contributes to fear of public speaking and interviewing is rambling and its counterparts—mansplaining and preaching. While mansplaining and preaching tend to be an underestimation of the audience's comprehension capabilities, rambling is usually due to nerves or lack of preparation. All cases can be treated by preparing your idea or example in a very specific way: A big picture, an idea, and an example. That's it. Ideally, each part should be one to two sentences. Not only does this save you from droning on and on, it is especially handy for TV interviews where journalists have to edit down to soundbites and can't include a 5-minute answer.

Say you're a social media manager and a question you often get asked is whether kids should be featured prominently on their influencer parents' pages. You would start with your big picture and flow right into your idea and example.

Big Picture: No, children should not be featured on their parents' pages until they're old enough to decide if they'd like that sort of attention.

Idea: The idea behind this is keeping children safe, not just from predators, but from bullying and harsh, damaging criticism from strangers.

Example: Rochelle Humes is a great example of this. Though she shared parts of her children's lives on her Instagram, she didn't show their faces until both girls asked to be a part of it.

When you have this format down, you could even take it a step further to add another example:

Example: When Beyoncé's daughter Blue's image was shared in the media, she was subject to several vicious attacks on her looks.

If your concept, idea, or point, can't quite be whittled into this format, try numbering. Start off by saying "I have three points on this," followed by a big picture of each point. This will help lead to a conversation or invite questions, while still keeping you on track.

Now, this doesn't mean this is all you'll say on a topic, but a clear, concise answer like this, usually opens the door for questions and a conversation that you can carry on with. This method is helpful across subjects with lofty ideology and with numbers as well. While you won't be able to prepare for every single question; nailing down the responses you give the most, allows you the brain space to quickly tackle other subjects and makes you well-rehearsed in answering questions this way. Again, you must practice.

Another thing that causes people to ramble is being afraid of silence. You made a great point, and you stopped talking, but your host or interviewer hasn't responded. So you continue talking just to fill that gap. Especially if you've already said what you have to say, this will only devolve into repetition or a lengthy rant.

We'll talk about how to handle repetition later, but in the case of silence, the first step is to not fear it. Don't let it lead you into scurrying to fill it. Instead, use a sentence to either encourage conversation or indicate that you're finished talking. If there are multiple people in the interview, you could ask, "anybody want to add to that?" or "are there any further considerations?". If it's just you and an interviewer you could say something like "I'll leave that there for now," or "That's my brief version of my thoughts on that."

Habit:
Trigger Words or Phrases (so, of course, that's a good question, well let me explain, or let me put that into context)

Solution:
Diversify your phrases, or OWN it

As I mentioned, this is one I'm especially guilty of. I said it so much my producers started making fun of me. In fact, when I coach in person, I treat my students to a video of me saying "*of course*" on 10 different interviews. Especially when I'm on a red carpet or the interview I have coming next is a surprise, I need a beat to allow me to quickly think up my next question. My '*of course*' is usually followed by a compliment or some other opening statement that warms my interviewee up and gives me some time. It serves me to have a trigger phrase. If you feel you need one too, you can try to diversify your phrase by practicing to insert another phrase or two in place of your regular one. Or, you can make it your thing. Now, when I say *'of course',* I say it with such energy and gusto that sometimes, my interviewees even say it back to me, energized to begin our chat. My producers expect it and my cameramen incorporate it. It's now as much a part of me as introducing myself to new guests. If you can and want to own your trigger phrase, go ahead and do so. You'd be surprised what you can pull off with a little confidence.

Habit:
Poor Eye Contact
Solution:
Find Your Focal Point

As we've learned, you can always ask where you should be looking if the person shooting doesn't give you a direction. But even when you know where to look, many struggle with maintaining eye contact. Although it's particularly important if you're going to be on camera, —in any interview at all—you should strive to maintain good eye contact to establish a connection with your host or audience. Good eye contact doesn't mean you need to pierce the soul of your interviewer with your eyes and never look away, but it does mean that at least 80% of the time, you should be looking at your focal point. React naturally. If you would normally look down at your hands when you're talking about something sad, or close your eyes when you're expressing a feeling of bliss, do that. Just always remember to return to your focal point as naturally as possible, to ensure that the audience and interviewer are connecting with you. If it's uncomfortable to look directly at a person, you can choose something in the background that is just slightly behind, or ever so slightly beside your interviewer. Avoid darting your eyes back and back and forth or focusing on anything in the background. Getting distracted is easy, but looking distracted by having your eyes going everywhere looks particularly unpolished. In today's world, we do a lot of virtual interviews. In this case, make sure you know exactly where your camera is, and look there. It's easy on an iPhone, for example, to look at yourself or the little box where the person you're speaking to is. What you'll find is that even though in this case, you think you're focused on the right place, the playback will have you looking off slightly, because the camera is to the left or right of the actual screen. If using your webcam, focus on the light that most computers have when they're recording, or use a tiny piece of colored tape to mark where you want to focus. Be careful not to cover the camera itself. You probably know what I'm going to say next: **practice**. So practice to tune out distractions by choosing a focal point and concentrating there.

Habit:
Misaddressing your interviewer
Solution:
Ask people how they wish to be addressed

This is one I see occurring so often, and what people don't realize is that in most cases, this is not bad manners, but simply a habit. We naturally resort to calling people what our first outward impressions of them are - Sir, Ma'am, Miss, Mrs, etc. But what we have to realize is that in today's world, people are pretty particular about their titles and pronouns, and it is at the minimum respectful to call people what they'd like to be called. As someone who has made the mistake of calling a recently divorced woman, 'Mrs', when she prefered 'Ms' and not addressing someone as 'Dr' after the years they spent in medical school, I'll tell you right now, it can cause embarrassment and discomfort on both ends. So how will you know what people want to be called? You ask them politely. "What would you prefer me to refer to you as?", "Is Mrs. okay with you, or would you prefer something else." Almost everybody would prefer to be asked than misaddressed. This principle also rings true for pronunciations of names. If you even have a sliver of doubt, it's best to ask. I once shot a profile of an artist who did a painting of an international soccer star. At the reveal, the two met and took photos and posed beside the beautiful work of art. Seconds later, as the soccer star was being interviewed by several stations, he said how grateful he was to the artist, someone he'd developed a bond with and respected deeply. It was a truly touching moment… except, he said the artists' name wrong. He said it wrong repeatedly. Now, what seemed to be a moment of genuine gratitude and respect seemed performative and shallow. After all, if you respect someone so much, wouldn't you know how to pronounce their name? Just like it is the journalist's job to spell your name right and get your title correctly in their story, it's also your responsibility to refer to them and anyone else you interact with correctly. If their name is tricky, try asking, "Will you pronounce your name for me? I want to make sure I get it right," or "This looks pretty straightforward, but I just want to make sure it's Seh-rah, and not Sah-rah." People will always appreciate the ask, and you will appreciate the security of knowing you won't look silly down the line.

Habit:
Repeating
Solution:
Say it a Different Way

There's something I learned in journalism school that changed my communication style in my everyday life. I have an accent. Having lived in America a third of my life, these days it's not as strong as it used to be. When I first got here as a teen however, my accent used to be really strong, and I got used to people asking me to repeat myself. I always assumed they didn't understand my accent, and would usually repeat exactly what I'd said louder and as clearly as I could. As my accent became more neutral both due to time and subtle changes for journalism purposes, I found that when people asked me to repeat, and I'd say the same thing, they still wouldn't understand. Did I need to sound more American? That made me uncomfortable, because although I had made subtle changes to my speech, I didn't want to erase my identity completely. That's when a professor told me that 85% of time, it wasn't that my accent was getting in the way, it's that my question or answer was unclear, and most people, to be polite, would simply ask me to repeat. At first, I didn't give much thought to it, but in later interviews, when someone asked me to repeat, instead of giving them the same words with higher energy, I rephrased and simplified my questions. To my surprise, the reactions were ones of gratitude and understanding, and the answers I got became more clear. If an interviewer asks you to repeat, sometimes, yes it could be because they didn't understand you, or couldn't hear you, but consider that they may be looking for you to rephrase or simplify your answer. Especially in a pre-recorded interview, simple and concise answers are usually best. Even now in everyday conversations, when people ask me to repeat, I deliver my answer differently to ensure my best shot at comprehension.

Habit:
Apologizing
Solution:
Pause or Wrap

We've seen it so many times. Someone goes off track, stumbles or forgets their train of thought and immediately starts apologizing. We hope we're getting people to be sympathetic to our perceived deficit but in actuality, drawing attention to a shortcoming only serves to make you look like an amateur. If you do find yourself rambling or stumbling, do *not* apologize. No utterances of 'I'm so sorry you guys," or "ugh, this sounds so stupid", or "what am I even saying. Is this even making sense?" or even make noises like "bleh bleh bleh." Pause, breathe and regroup, or wrap it up neatly with no apologies by saying something like, "I could continue, but I'd love to pause here and see what questions you may have."

If you haven't heard me say it enough, practice is key here. Maybe more so with this particular session than any other. I'm sure you've heard somewhere that it takes 21 days to form or break a habit. I'm not sure how accurate the number is, however I am sure that these changes don't happen overnight. Identify if any of these habits belong to you and work on replacing them with more productive habits.

Chapter 7
The Interview Itself

 If you dare to jump into the spotlight, you better be ready to dance.

– *Jeff Lee*

We've learned about the media, pitched our interview, gotten noticed, prepared, gotten physical, and now we're *finally* at the interview. You made it! Well, almost… We still have to deliver. So what's important to remember at and during your interview? Luckily, if you've prepped right, not too much, but here are a few things you definitely want to keep in mind.

Assume everything you say can be heard and seen

That's right. Whether you have a mic on or not, whether your Zoom has started or it hasn't, if you think you've clicked mute or you think your camera is on or not - even if they've cut to a commercial break - assume the person on the other end whether live or virtual, can hear and see you. This goes for before, during and after an interview. The last thing you want is for all your hard work to go down the drain because of an off-key comment, an inappropriate joke or, or even a fart. Yes, a fart. One only has to Google 'Zoom Fails' to see the multitude of things that can happen when one forgets or fails to recognize that they're live. Therefore, from the moment you set foot in the studio, start your video call or pick up your telephone, you're on the record. Which brings me to my next point…

Don't go off the record

We've seen it in movies and pop-culture, and even heard it in business settings and casual scenes—"this is off the record." Except, it's not. Similarly to assuming that you can be seen and heard at all times, assume that everything you say and do will be reported. If you're thinking, 'but Rae, you said most journalists weren't trying to make us look bad,' you'd be right. We're not, and we probably won't, but at the end of the day our duty is to our audience and to the story. Unless you have a very close relationship with a journalist who you trust and have established a deep mutual understanding that they won't use certain soundbites, ideas or material; it's best to keep anything you don't want heard to yourself. From personal experience, the worst thing is when someone goes 'off the record' to you after an interview and reveals something that will make your story incorrect, untruthful or even irrelevant in a day or two. If a journalist asks you to say or disclose something you aren't comfortable revealing, feel free to decline using the techniques found in Chapter 8 (Controversial Questions).

Greet Everybody

This seems like just basic manners, but even the best of us can forget our graces when we're in a high pressure situation. Be sure to be natural and polite to everyone - the camera crew, the make up artists, production assistants, front desk, associate producers and anyone else you may come across. In media, it usually takes an entire team, and most producers are protective of their pods. Your reputation is also majorly important in this industry as nobody wants to work with someone unpleasant or ungrateful. Remember that the goal here is to forge relationships so that getting media attention later on is easier. Every single journalist can remember the stars who have been pleasant *and* unpleasant to us. I spoke to entertainment journalist and comedian Michael Yo about why this particular piece of advice is important. If you're an entertainment junkie like I am, you may have a special connection to the name Michael Yo because he commanded E! News as one of their top correspondents, as well as a few other major outlets before crossing over to the other side of the mic when he went fully after his passion of comedy. Michael has interviewed *everybody*, so believe him when he says, "the interview starts from the moment you interact." "How you act, how you perform, how you treat others during your interview means a lot to other people, because they're going to talk about you too," Michael told me. "It's the most important thing. I'm going to just bring up a couple names: Will Smith, The Rock, Kevin Hart," he cited as examples of stars with impeccable interview etiquette. "Will Smith comes in and shakes everybody's hand: camera guy's hand, the audio person's hand. He says hi to every single person. The Rock does that, Kevin Hart does that. And those are the most successful people. An interview is just an extension of who you truly are," Michael says. Now if Will Smith can give everybody his best, so can you. But not only is this a simple matter of manners and networking. Michael says that for the celebs that go out of their way to be polite and personable, he wants to give them 100% in his interviews with them. That means maybe that one word you mispronounced, they may give you the chance to shoot it again, or they may ask you to rephrase something on the phone. It may just be that they reflect your good energy and in turn your interview goes really smoothly. "The more you see these people, the more they will fight for you. Basically it all comes down to being a good human being. If you're a good human being, it will come back around to you," Michael says. It's just so important to be nice.

Be Present

Another one that almost seems silly to mention, but is well worth bringing up. You've prepared, and you're ready. Don't seem distant or out of touch by trying to remember every single talking point or be overly fixated on the process. Be present. "When you do get interviewed, it's an extension of you. Whatever project you're putting out into the world, you want people to be able to see it," Michael advises. So you want to be sure to get enough energy before so you're alert and you can tune in to your surroundings. My colleague, Xixi Yang, an award-winning entertainment journalist who has interviewed everyone from Lizzo to Oprah, emphasized being present as a way to keep your interview focused. "Focus on why you're doing the interview. I've interviewed people where they have projects to promote but I keep on having to direct the conversation 'cuz they're all over the place," Xixi said.

Remember Your Audience

This one is especially important for influencers and people who create their own content on their own platforms and are used to running their own show. Once you're interviewing with an outlet, be mindful that you're in somebody else's house. Just as how you wouldn't go to someone else's house and put your feet on the furniture, you want to be careful to keep within the parameters of their rules and their audience. "Many fail because they lack the professionalism that's required of different networks and their audience," Xixi said. "On your YouTube you can swear etc, but that's not the case on national television. Think in terms of your audience. Who is your audience that you're trying to get with your messaging? For you to come across as authentic, effective and someone that you'd want to listen to - someone engaging - you have to be real and in order to be real you have to understand who you're talking to. Your stories will need to resonate with this audience." When we talked about pitching, we discussed sharing how you could serve the outlet's audience. Don't forget that in the live interview - especially if it's not a personality interview. "A lot of influencers have built a business on being who they are, which is amazing, but they haven't yet found how they can use their talent to service other people," Xixi said. "Their interviews tend to sound more like "this is what I'm doing. Me, me, me… all eyes on me. You have to be thinking about the audience."

Start light hearted

Yes, even if you're a doctor going in to talk about something extremely grim, start off light. This doesn't mean you have to crack a joke or be super smiley—you can gauge what light behavior is appropriate for your subject matter—but especially in a live interview or a situation where you didn't get to interact with your interviewer ahead of time, you want to establish a rapport of trust and comfort. "Always make the person interviewing you feel welcome," Michael advises. "The more welcome and fun they have, the better the interview. And let's be honest, the whole purpose of an interview is for people to see you in a light that you want them to see you in. I've seen the celebrities that I look up to say, 'my job is to make the interviewer look great so when they get back to work they'll be like 'you got a great interview!'" The spotlight is on you, but at the interview itself, it's also about them in the sense that they are the other half of your high five.

Get your key message in early

Although we've discussed how to prepare and your messaging, you want to remember not to linger too long on the pleasantries and introductions, or build up for too long. Especially in a television interview where you want to lean into being conversational, make sure you get your key message in early. Another reason to want to do this? Because anything can happen. And I mean *anything*. I once produced a morning show where we lost electrical power two minutes into the segment. Although we stayed on air, with lights going out and panic in the background (yep, I definitely panicked), it was really hard to stay focused for the rest of that interview. If you can pull it off and show grace under pressure, that's excellent. But at the very minimum, you want to make sure that just in case your interview gets cut short, even by a little, that you got your key message across.

Finish Strong

Just as important as how you begin, is how you end. Make sure that you end on a high note both with your message and your energy. Again, a high note doesn't mean all of a sudden finding a silver lining after a grim message, but you'll want to end on something strong and impactful or perhaps even with giving your interviewer, and thus your audience, something to think about. It makes my life so easy as a journalist when someone gives me the perfect sound bite to end on. Of course, don't forget to say thank you to your interviewer and the team as you're leaving!

Offer a point of contact

Chances are you've been in communication with someone from the team, but feel free to offer a point of contact to a member of the team if appropriate. If you don't get a chance to do it in person, send an email to your point of contact with an extra thank you and offering your information should they ever need it again. I've dug many business cards out of the bottom of my camera bag for later stories when a person who'd given me their card popped into my head.

Once your interview is over (and you've given your thanks!), pat yourself on the back! I can guarantee you that your producers or interviewers will be running along to the next thing, but there are a few things you'll want to do as well before the interview goes live and after it has run.

- *Get a copy of the interview and use social media to interact* - Let people know you're going to be featured! It helps both you and the outlet get visibility. Be sure to ask if you can share any behind the scenes or clips you took, and if you don't have those, tools like Canva can help you create something eye catching simply and and quickly.

- *Follow up with helpful resources and information - NOT an ask* - Producers and journalists don't take kindly to guests asking to change, omit or correct things - especially if the interview hasn't even run yet. Remember, this is their job and they know what they're doing. If you have prepped and done your part, they will present you as you appeared—in your best light. Also wait at least until your interview has run before you start asking about further opportunities and interviews (unless there is a really obvious opening or opportunity). I can't tell you how many people want a second interview before the first has even aired. If you're great, you'll get more, don't worry. What you can opt to do if it is relevant, is be open to offering further resources and information. For a lot of stories that I do, I need to reach out for clarifying details to enhance the story. I once had a person tell me they didn't feel like doing anything that day and therefore couldn't answer my simple question for *their* feature. If you see another story you think that the producer or outlet would be interested in, feel free to suggest it. Most journalists love a good tip or resource - especially if it comes from a person they trust.

- *Keep up with your interviews* - Once your interview is out, don't forget to add it to your website, social pages, or at least keep track of what you've done. If you've ever heard that it's easier to get a job while you have a job, that principal applies here too. Especially if you're positioning yourself as an expert in your subject area, having a portfolio, even one or two pieces of press to show, opens your chances a bit more.

- *Study your own interview* - You knew this one was coming! Watch and audit your interview. Read your article. Listen to your radio interview. How did you look? How was your energy? Were your eyes darting? Be honest, but fair with yourself especially if you're new to interviewing. Hardly anyone nails everything in an interview, but if you do the biggest things well, nobody will even notice. Practice what you're weak at and don't be afraid to let a confidante tell you what vibe they got from your interview.

Check out Spotlight Swag (chapter 10) for an Interview Review checklist where you can get a quick snapshot of all the things you should be looking for.

Chapter 8
Controversial Questions and Negative Press

It is always a risk to speak to the press: they are likely to report what you say

– Hubert H. Humphrey

At some point in your stay in the spotlight, the inevitable happens. Your company gets accused of something shady. You go through a relationship scandal that has reflected upon your brand. You misspeak or are misquoted, or even misunderstood, and you receive backlash. We've all seen the paparazzi crowding an embattled celebrity hurling questions at them while their team shields them and they keep their eyes straight ahead in silence. Even if you're not a celebrity, and you don't have a crowd, these bad moments happen to the best of us. It may not even be a bad moment. It may be something as simple as a controversial question you didn't expect. I, for example, was once sent to cover a pork event for Jamaica's first ever Food and Drink Festival. There was every type of pork you could think of,--fried, baked, jerked, candied. There was pork cheese, pork sushi, and even dessert topped with bacon sauce. As a big foodie, and in particular a very proud pork lover, I was excited for this event. That is right up until my producer forwarded me several articles condemning the consumption of red meat with a list of questions for the organizers. The questions all summed up to asking, 'If red meat is so harmful to eat, why would you put society at risk with a whole festival celebrating it'. Before I went through the door, I got a reminder to make sure I asked the questions. 'Don't chicken out,' it said. Pun definitely intended. Once there, I pulled aside a friend that worked for the brand and told him I had to ask that tough question. I didn't want to blindside his boss and I didn't want the brand to look bad, but my boss was right - the question had to be asked. He was able to put together a sophisticated and simple answer to feed his boss before I went in for the interview and all was well. The problem is, however, you will hardly ever get that courtesy. In an interview that seems straightforward and even fun, you may get a curveball about a current event that affects the topic or a rogue question that the reporter thought of on the stop. You can't always prepare for the exact question, but you can prepare a strategy to ensure that you come off looking the best you possibly can. While I can't speak for every reporter or publication, - as I've mentioned before, there are some bad eggs out there - rarely do reporters ask you questions because they *want* to make you look bad. Do they want the truth? Yes. Do they want to satisfy a query that will inform the public? Yes. Do they sometimes get instructions from higher-ups to ask an uncomfortable question? Yes. Can you sometimes look bad in the process of responding? *Definitely yes.* Reporters' tactics aren't all the same either. Some may slide the question in. Some may ask it outright. Some may be cheeky. There are even some who will try to get an emotional reaction out of you because that's what they need for their story that day. But if you understand that the reporter wants this to go well, as badly as you do; it will help you have a clear enough mind to approach a negative question with grace. Before we get into exactly how to answer negative questions, there are a few core things to remember:

You don't have to comment, but 'no comment' *is* a comment

I want to make this clear: You don't have to answer questions you don't want to answer or are not equipped or have adequate information to answer. Your best choice however, is to turn these questions into opportunities to change the subject, redirect the conversation or insert a light moment. None of these happen when you say 'no comment.'

Michael Yo, who we heard from in the previous chapter, 'The Interview Itself', has experienced having to ask the hard questions millions of times. "They're doing their job," Michael says of reporters. "If you're at an interview and you just broke up with whoever, nobody wants to interview you for five minutes about your movie. Our job is to find pop culture bits that people want to watch. We're not malicious and we're not trying to come after you, but we have to ask these questions because that's our job. Your job is to say you don't want to answer it - and then guess what? The stress is off both of us!" If you think it's as easy as saying no comment or just stating that you don't want to answer it and moving along, you haven't been paying attention so far. No comment *is* a comment, and since we're building our media currency here, we want to give the reporter something to work with while looking good ourselves. At times, publications will reach out to ask questions about whatever controversy you're involved in. No comment is not great here either, because it allows readers or viewers to concoct their own ideas. Later on, we'll talk through some 'Controversial Questions and Negative Press Prompts' to help you find the best ways to answer questions that warrant 'no comment'.

If you react, we 'win'.

I say win with air quotes because, again, 'we', the media, most likely aren't trying to trip you up. However, in a society where people constantly pit the media against their subjects; it will likely be perceived that way. No good journalist will stop you either if you start to ruin yourself - especially if it's live. As painful as it may be for some of us, we have to let you talk and tell your story. Unless you're a pro and extremely witty, a quick reaction usually manifests as lashing out, saying something derogatory, making a false statement, or even in extreme cases, walking out, and is usually a win for those who want to see you fail. A quick reaction may also lead to you contradicting yourself, your brand or your image.

I can remember an interview my mentor Anthony conducted in 2016 with Grammy nominated reggae artist, Etana. Etana, then known as a vocal supporter of black rights, roots and culture and an unofficial ambassador for the working class, came on our show *Entertainment Report* to talk about the recent birth of her daughter, body positivity and her new music. When questioned on her political views for the upcoming US election - the hot topic at the time - Etana proudly declared 'Yes, I am a Trump supporter,' and proceeded to explain her reasons for liking him, including that the then-presidential candidate was frank and outspoken, much like herself. Now, of course, everyone is free to support who they want, and certainly free to state what they believe in, but this seemed to be very off brand for someone who was a champion for some of the things Trump seemed to berate. Any good journalist would see a story here and keep pressing, and that's exactly what Anthony did. When he pointed out some of the discrepancies in her brand and Trump's beliefs, she immediately jumped into defensive mode and provided a reaction that would go on to become Jamaican TV gold. She rambled answers filled with misinformation and a poorly informed point of view, including accusing Trump's wife Melania of being a non-white 'Mexican who could barely speak English'. This interview was officially no longer about her baby, it was about her beliefs. Beliefs that she would have more than likely been prepared to defend in a much more polished way had she approached the initial question better. It became a back and forth and her feature eventually became a profile of her prejudice. Led by a few questions, she did most of the talking, eventually declaring, 'my music has nothing to do with what I believe in'. She went on to say, 'because I am a Trump supporter [this] has nothing to do with what I sing about or what I write about.' After intense backlash, Etana would later go on to accuse our show of twisting her words and clipping her quotes; further endangering her image as she squared off against a reputed journalist. Etana would eventually recover and admit to another journalist, "I just shouldn't have — I now know that especially when you're talking about politics, you need to know it *all*. You need to know as much as possible. About both sides; both people. And if you think you know enough, read some more." Etana could have prevented this conversation from becoming controversial by stalling her reaction and not allowing herself to be drawn out.

Be upfront *before* the interview if there's something you absolutely won't answer

In a similar controversy about political stance, Stacey Dash, an actress from the iconic film *Clueless*, faced intense scrutiny for her conservative political beliefs. Her career spun into political prominence when she decided to face the backlash and hold firm on her viewpoints, encouraging other people to be the same. Dash never backed down, usually very forthcoming with the source of her opinions. She appeared as a guest on many political commentary shows, and was the target of many reports, rumors and ridicule across the 2012 election cycle. Unfortunately, years after, that's what Dash became known for. Especially after being plagued by some trouble in her personal life, Dash became a target for stirring the pot and the Antichrist of black liberals; no matter the project or the positive message she had, the media focused on what they knew was the story people wanted to hear: Stacey's political opinion.

So how do you move on from that and promote your new projects and even new viewpoints when that's all people want to hear about? You take the possibility of the conversation out of the question. And that's exactly what Stacey did. At first, she started limiting her interviews altogether. At events she'd attend, she took pictures on the Red Carpet, but did not give interviews. While she still expressed her opinions on her social media, she was tight about using any other platform than her own space to say what she wanted to. In 2020, Clueless, the movie that skyrocketed Dash to fame, turned 25 and everybody was talking about it. When Dash agreed to an in-person interview with my outlet, I was very surprised, as I hadn't seen her do much press. Even more so, news had broken about her divorce from her 4th husband, just about nine months before she'd been arrested in a domestic violence incident with said husband AND, the US was in the middle of a global pandemic that had also become a bitter political war in an election year. But here was Stacey Dash, willing to give an interview. Before I could ask, my producer said, "here's the deal. No political questions, no personal questions. What we're talking about is Clueless. We've agreed; no questions unrelated to 'Clueless.'" Do you know what I felt in that moment? Relief. I wanted to talk about 'Clueless' and have a chance to ask Stacey everything I eventually did get to ask her: What was the first day on set like? What was the chemistry with the cast? What was it like playing a teenager when you were a grown woman with a baby? You know, the fun stuff! But how could I possibly focus on any of that when the issue of politics and her personal affairs were what people would want to hear? She made it easy, she took away that option. She didn't do it five seconds before the interview either. It was known well in advance, and we had the opportunity to decline the interview if we weren't interested in the subject matter she was open to discussing. Although I didn't ask her any questions about the intimate details of her personal struggles; towards the end of the interview I did mention that I noticed on her Instagram that she'd been away from LA a lot, and out in nature. She volunteered that she was taking time to reframe, refocus and concentrate on Christianity, and that she'd been pursuing her passion of interior design. She had to change her narrative somehow, and this was her way of doing it. This was not the first time I had heard of 'do not asks' from celebrity interviewees.

When interviewing Lamar Odom and then-new girlfriend Sabrina, his reps asked that we not ask any questions about Khloe Kardashian, his previous relationship that had been the overarching theme of his last few years of press. Again, I was glad. There was so much more to talk about: his stint on dancing with the stars, his new relationship, his desire to do public speaking. Real Housewives of New Jersey Teressa Guidice requested we not speak about the trouble in her family life in a 2019 interview. Respecting her wishes, we had a fun conversation, where she eventually, carefully did give me a few details on the state of her family, knowing I'd allow her to say as little or as much as she wished. Even if you're not a celebrity, most reputable reporters will respect your desire to not speak on a certain topic, or decline the interview altogether. If there is something you're trying to avoid, but you still want to get on with your life, do careful research on the outlet or the interviewer, make sure they're trustworthy, and be upfront about what you're not willing to say.

So what is the best way to answer an uncomfortable or controversial question? You redirect. That way, you decline to answer, keep the conversation moving and keep on target all in once. Redirecting is especially handy when you've been ambushed by the question, but if you know you have something controversial happening in your life or to your brand or project, have a redirection statement handy. Most methods of redirection start with acknowledgment. Acknowledgement doesn't necessarily mean agreement, it just means that you are recognizing the interviewers statement or question before shifting to what you want to talk about. It helps the redirection from seeming too abrupt or revealing that you're really escaping the question. Once you have acknowledged, you follow with a conjunction like 'but', and then your redirection statement - what you'd really like to focus on. A great example would be my pork event I previously mentioned. If the interviewer asked, 'haven't there been a lot of studies recently indicating that red meat, pork included, is really bad for you?' An answer of acknowledgement could say **'Yes**, there have been a lot of studies citing that as an issue **but** today, we celebrate the diverse ways that you can cook and consume red meat so that if you choose to indulge, you have a plethora of options.' This then opens the door for you to talk about the diverse offerings. You can focus on the healthiest ones to keep it consistent, for example, 'One of our talented chefs came up with bacon jam. Using half a teaspoon on your toast gives incredible flavor without the calories and risk of several slices of bacon.'

Often, an interviewer will offer a question based in public opinion or common opinion perhaps as a direct challenge to your viewpoint. In this case, especially if you're drowning or the topic is getting too heavy, you want to shift the focus completely. For example, if an interviewer hit Etana with, 'You support Trump and you're an immigrant. Doesn't Trump hate immigrants?' She could answer with, 'That's an opinion that a lot of people hold. What I'm focused on right now is taking care of my kid so that she grows up in a world where she can freely hold her own opinion.' You could then transition into talking about your child. 'Every day I look at her and I want her to be capable of independent thought so she can have lively discussions like this. Here's what I do with her…' Again, it started with acknowledgement, but this time the shift is a little more apparent and should signal to the interviewer that it's time to move on, because if they don't, they may come across as combative. Here are a few other prompts to help you redirect:

That's an issue **but…**

Some say that, **here's what I'm focused on…**

That's surely one opinion, **but let's look at this picture…**

People definitely argue about this one. **What I love is…**

I love that we're having this discussion, **but before we run out of time…**

There's some research that says that, **but here's what I'm an expert in…**

And what if you don't want to answer at all? Like we've spoken about, no comment indeed says a whole lot. Saying no, however, is easier than you think. Here are a few polite ways to do it that actually employ a similar strategy as the one we just discussed. Instead of acknowledgement here, you *express gratitude,* followed by a personal element, and then the **redirection**. For example, if I had violated our understanding and asked Stacey Dash about her recent divorce, she could have said something like, '*I appreciate you wanting to know that* Rae, **but I'd hate to ruin a celebration of Clueless with my own personal details.**' If appropriate, you can even push them along with a *tempting tidbit or question* - something like, *'Do you want to hear about the first scene we shot on the movie?'* In some cases, you can even add ***acknowledgement*** to the gratitude. If I had indeed asked Lamar Odom about Khloe Kardashian, he could say something like, "*Thanks for asking that question, I know a lot of people have questions about our relationship and* **you're a great reporter for asking that but I have so much to tell you about Dancing with the Stars.** Did you see last week?'

If you are a playful person, or can get away with being playful or cheeky, you can even poke some fun at the reporter for asking an out of bounds question.

My favorite example of this is when *The Hills* alum, Lauren Conrad, as part of an interview segment, had to pick a question out of a hat. The question read 'what's your favorite position?' - in reference to the bedroom. After a beat, Conrad replied, 'CEO,' with a playful smile. It was a perfect response, got her out of the hot seat, and ended up going viral for its cleverness. While I do love a great witty response, be careful with this one. I know we've all seen interviews with celebs that 'clapback' at reporters for asking them inappropriate questions. Again, unless the question is really, truly inappropriate, and not just the reporter asking a tough question in the name of their job, try to keep it light and polite. I can't stress enough that we're building media currency here.

Handling negative questions isn't the easiest thing. If it happens often enough because you're either facing a significant controversy, or you've gotten to a point in your career where you're the object of affection; some of this will roll off your back. Otherwise, put in some practice and think carefully about what your best response could be, if you ever have to face the music.

Spotlight Swag:
Psst! Want a few more prompts to help with preparing for negative press? Check out Chapter 10.

Part three

HAPPILY EVER INTERVIEW

Chapter 9
Do as the Stars Do

> *A horse never runs so fast as when he has other horses to catch up and outpace*
>
> – Ovid

As you've probably realized, I've come across many stars and celebrities during my time as an entertainment reporter and producer. From A-List to up-and-coming, each star has brought a different interview style with new lessons and details. Even the stars I haven't yet met are fun to watch from afar as other journalists interview them. I'm always asked who my favorite and least favorite stars are to interview and what they're 'really like' when the cameras aren't rolling. While I'm hesitant to ever name a worst -- after all, they're humans who have good days and bad days -- I will say there are highlights from many celebs that I think master the universal principles of giving a good interview. Besides practice, one of my favorite ways to learn something is to watch someone else do it. We look up tutorials on YouTube all the time for everything from sewing, to make-up, to math. Watching the stars do what they do is no different. Here are a few of my favorite stars along with what gives their interviews the x-factor. Some I've interviewed personally, and some I've watched on TV, or even as they were interviewed right in front of me. We've discussed most of the must-dos for interviews, but it's super helpful to watch the professionals do them. Feel free to look them up and study to see what lessons you can take from their interview styles. Oh, and there are pictures!

Kill 'Em With Kindness

A lot of networks hold events each year where they bring together cast members from an array of their shows for a long, but exciting, press day or week. They're usually a ton of fun but ultimately exhausting. One particular press tour, I was especially excited to interview Rosario Dawson. I'd long admired her as she always had impactful things to say and interesting projects to discuss. Plus of course, she's drop dead gorgeous. At the time her new series, Briarpatch, was on the network's line up and the entire cast was on the schedule for late in the afternoon. Having been there since 6:30am, late afternoon was a challenge. Red Carpets aren't as easy or seamless as they look. Agents and managers decide who gets an interview. There's a hierarchy for interviews as well. Getting snubbed is something you learn not to take offense to, and making nice with agents and managers and sticking to their guidelines is a must-do because they are your ticket to your interview. I hate to say it, but my experience is that minorities get snubbed more than others. On that particular press day where we were expecting Rosario, we had a decent place on the carpet and had had a really successful day of interviews. Things got a little delayed and when the Briarpatch cast ended up on the carpet a little later than planned, a lot of media houses had already started packing up. Not me though. That was the interview I wanted. She started making her way down the carpet and as she was talking to the outlet in front of me, her press personnel came to let me know that unfortunately, she was stopping there. I was crestfallen. I'd waited all day and I was so close. I begged her. I'd keep it short - one question only - but it was a firm no. I stood my ground anyway. I would leave after she did when I knew there was absolutely zero chance.

Rosario wrapped up her interview and her press people started to guide her (and my hopes) off the carpet, Rosario glanced back. There were 3 outlets left and I saw the glimmer in her eyes three seconds before she broke away from her people and sprinted ever so elegantly directly towards me. She landed in front of me with a giant hug and I immediately said 'Thank you so much. You are the best, I'll keep it short.' I spit out a question and she answered it with as much detail and dedication as she'd done for everybody else. It was a moment I'll never forget and one I appreciated from the bottom of my heart, because she didn't have to do it. She was the celebrity and having just done a string of interviews with much bigger outlets, she didn't need to do mine -- but she did. That kind of kindness and grace is an invaluable interview skill. I've come to realize that most industries have a cycle of up and down. Sometimes people need you and sometimes you need people. If you've built a great relationship with the press - which doesn't take much - they'll be there for you too. Kindness comes across in your interviews and is a great base for relationship building. If Rosario Dawson's career should ever decline and she calls me 50 years from now for an interview, I've got her!

Another person who is an absolute joy to interview because of the kindness factor is David Arquette. I've now interviewed him several times for projects that were his own, as well as while a guest at other premieres. He's always willing to take the time to interview and spend enough time to give you quality answers and thank you - genuinely - for your time. Not to mention he's always down for a photo. As professional as we aim to be, sometimes we just want a good old fashioned fan photo. It's nice when a personality is kind enough to allow you to even ask that.

Let Your Light Shine

I think it's safe to say Sofia Vergara was not having a great day when I interviewed her. Everyone was wary as a pandemic was looming; though we were not on shut down nor knew to distance yet. It was extremely hot outside where the interviews were taking place in peak sun, and the shrill screams from the crowd weren't helpful either. As she walked in to tape America's Got Talent, Sofia was dressed in a gown that looked extremely tight and of course, tv make-up which tends to be heavy and is often not sweat-proof. Yet, if you watch our interview from that day you would never have known. Sofia was armed with energy and the vibrance that she's known for and knew when to turn it on for the camera. Sometimes you have to dig deep to find it.

Another thing I love about her is that, like me, she has an accent. So many people have told me they are shy to speak up because of their accent whether it be regional or language based. Their shyness affects their energy and their interviews turn out looking poor. An accent is nothing to be ashamed of or nothing to hide behind. In most cases it may be an even bigger reason to project more energy. If you feel your accent is affecting your clarity, practice can fix that, but most times, you sound just fine.

Charm and Disarm

If you've watched American Idol or America's Got Talent, you may think Simon Cowell is mean, rude or pompous and full of attitude, especially after the controversy between him and former America's Got Talent judge Gabrielle Union. Maybe he is. However, based on my interactions with him on the Red Carpet (prior to those accusations), there are valuable takeaways from his camera-facing behavior. My nerves struck like no other when it was time to interview Simon. After all, he'd given so many a boost in their careers, who wouldn't want to impress him. My nerves quickly melted away however, when the first thing out of his mouth was an acknowledgment that I was new to reporting on the show, a genuine compliment and a thank you for being a part of the Red Carpet that day. Throughout the interview, his answers were sincere, thoughtful, and at the end he thanked me once again for taking part and shook my hand. And it wasn't just that he was feeling nice that day, on subsequent red carpets, he remembered who I was and led with the same charm that disarmed my nerves and made the interview flow so much better. If you can put the person interviewing you at ease and make them comfortable; I promise your interview will go that much better.

A HEAP of Authenticity

We've spoken about authenticity many times throughout the book, and of course have gone in detail about

HEAP; but to underline this concept I want to point out a celebrity who merges both well and whose very success is arguably based on her authenticity. While she's not someone I've personally interviewed (she's on my wishlist!), anyone who has watched an interview with Cardi B can see that she is herself 100% of the time. It doesn't mean it doesn't get her in trouble from time to time, and it doesn't mean that she's perfect. However it does mean that her audience and her detractors alike know exactly what they're getting and are endeared to her in some way. She also brings a humble brag, energy, action and a personal touch to every single interview. She is consistent in her energy and vibe across every interview and every platform, and it's clear that it's not because she tries hard. If you're simple and frank, be simple and frank. If you're loud and over the top, be loud and over the top. Cardi B proves there are ways to do this within the parameters of good interview etiquette. A favorite of mine was Cardi's interview for Vogue's 73 Questions, a candid style interview series where the producer follows the celebrity around asking them a string of questions at random. From her grandmother's humble home in the Bronx, holding her sleeping toddler, and therefore talking at a slightly lower decibel than we're accustomed to; Cardi still manages to bring across her full personality, welcoming the audience 'to the hood' and managing to endear us to her modest beginnings and the hardships of motherhood. She brings energy with her signature facial expressions, language, curse words and noises (still holding the sleeping child). When she finally puts the baby down, she introduces action at the prompt of the interviewer, by calling her husband and engaging in some playful banter and highlighting her accomplishments. All in all, knowing who you are and sticking to that, makes your HEAP phenomenally stronger.

The Real Housewives of Redirection

I'll never forget the first time an interview of mine was redirected. On the side of the interviewer, journalist or producer, a well done redirection means you have no choice but to follow the interviewee's subtle lead to mitigate the risk of making yourself look like an amateur or a bully. Interestingly, the personalities I've found to do this best are the Real Housewives. Across the franchise, I've probably interviewed about 7 or 8 of the women, each with their own distinct way of doing things. The first one to redirect me was Phaedra Parks. We were at a gala to raise awareness for drug abuse and while I started with the first few must-get formal questions - why she was supporting this event, her message to young people,etc., I proceeded to ask her about the Real Housewives where there'd recently been some controversy involving her. Whether it was that she genuinely didn't feel like speaking about it or adding fire to the flames or she felt like we should have stuck to the topic of the Gala, Phaedra flawlessly redirected by saying, 'Rae, I appreciated that show but the Real Housewives will not be my legacy.' Now I was curious. Wasn't that show her biggest claim to fame? She practically dictated my next question - what would her legacy be? From there, she proceeded to let me know a few of the projects she was working on and tied the last one back to where we were standing and what we were doing there. I know delving back into any drama would just make me look like a jerk, so I continued our conversation and ended up getting a fantastic interview where I and my audience alike would learn way more facts about Phaedra than ever before (she is both an attorney and a mortician). I'd never had somebody lead my interview like that and it was a helpful learning experience as a journalist. Phaedra would not be the last Housewife cast member to redirect me, though she certainly was the most graceful about it (or maybe I learned and got better at focusing my interviews). Either way, they are some of the best celebrities to watch in trying to avoid controversial topics.

Virtually Perfect

If you're reading this, that means you likely made it through the year 2020. Congratulations! If you somehow skipped 2020 and are reading this decades after, let me tell you this: it was a hot mess. The world as we know it got flipped upside down in every single way, including the media industry. Red carpets turned into online press events, living rooms became studios and the coveted one-on-ones were conducted via telephone, often in cars hiding from one's kids / roommates / pets. It was a disaster, but a disaster that reminded us media folk how to readjust, and showed the folks on the other end of the camera and mic just what they were capable of. Zoom everything became the norm, including press interviews, and several celebrities simply nailed the new practice. Bonus points: we got to see inside their homes. My favorite to watch: None other than Jennifer Lopez. While JLO can generally do no wrong in my eyes, I paid particular attention to her Zoom etiquette. First there were her backdrops - various rooms in her home, her garden, her gym, her living room. Her outfits always acknowledged she was in her home, but also not giving up on glamor. Whoever framed her interviews generally did a great job of making sure we could see and hear her well. And, of course, she brought her bubbly personality and passion for her work straight across that computer screen. While there's a tolerance for the oopsies and the upsets that come with doing your professional work from home; as online interviews get embedded into the culture, it's important to set yourself up for success. Celeb zoom interviews will remain live on the internet for your review for a long time to come.

The stars above aren't the only ones to learn from. A quick Google search will reveal all the interviews you could ever hope for, and new ones pop up each and every day. Doesn't have to be celebrities either. 'Regular' people give good interviews you can learn from too. As you watch, check in with yourself and notice your gut reaction to an interview. Note things you like and want to adopt. Did you like the simplicity of their Zoom background? The confidence in their voice? The way they bantered with the interviewer? There's always something.

Chapter 10
Spotlight Swag

Knowledge is of no value unless you put it into practice.

– Anton Chekhov

Throughout the book, I've referenced lists, acronyms, mnemonics and more to help you get a grip on this media thing. This chapter contains simplified versions of the resources, as well as additional ones to help you practice and refine your skills. And don't forget, watching interviews on TV and sites like YouTube are a phenomenal way to observe and take note, especially when combined with the skills in this book.

Pitch Checklist

Use this checklist before sending a pitch to a journalist or producer.

- ☐ *Professional Email Address*
- ☐ *Correct Contact Name*
- ☐ *Tailored Pitch*
- ☐ *Short and Sweet*
- ☐ *Catchy Subject Line*
- ☐ *Punchy First Sentence*
- ☐ *Contact Info*
- ☐ *Proofread and Spell Check*

Pitch Templates

No idea what to write in your pitch? Use the template below for a head start and the examples afterwards to show how you can personalize them. Don't forget to attach your support materials!

Hi [NAME]

My name is [YOUR NAME] and I am [YOUR TITLE]. I've been [WATCHING / READING / LISTENING TO] [PROGRAM / OUTLET] and I thought my perspective on [PITCH TOPIC] may interest you.

I have [HUMBLE BRAG]. In the past I have [EXAMPLES]. We could make this segment interactive and interesting by [ACTION].

I'm passionate about this because [PERSONAL]

If we align, please feel free to contact me at [CONTACT INFORMATION]

I have attached some resources for your perusal.

Looking forward to hearing from you!

[Name]

Hi John,

My name is Dr. Aleah Francis and I am an allergist at the MedStar Regional Hospital in Newark. I've been reading Thursday Healthline in The Chronicle and I thought my perspective on allergy management may interest you.

I have a decade of experience in allergy and immunology and have been focusing on allergies local to our area. I can give practical examples of how to best stay allergy free. What's more is we could make this interactive and interesting by providing beautiful illustrations you can publish. My patients always benefit greatly from seeing this drawn out.

I know this is the time of year where allergies are rampant in our city. I'm sure you or someone you know has fallen victim at some point and I'd love to help!

I've attached some resources for your perusal.

If we align, please feel free to contact me at 787.385.4938 or at this email address

Looking forward to hearing from you!

Aleah

Hi Lizzie,

My name is Rae Williams and I am a Journalist and Media Presence Strategist. I've been watching Wake Up with Wendy on Instagram Live and I thought my perspective on the basics of breaking through in media may interest you.

I have a decade of experience in media and have interviewed personalities I know your audience will love. From Sofia Vergara to Sting, I can take your audience on a brief journey of how to put their best media foot forward. What's more is we could make this segment interactive and interesting by playing one of my 'Media Mogul' practice games with your host Wendy.

Wendy and I actually worked together years ago when we were both starting our careers at TVJ. To connect years later would be fun, entertaining and a solid example to viewers that the sky's the limit for women of color in media.

I've attached some resources for your perusal.

If we align, please feel free to contact me at 787.385.4938 or at this email address

Looking forward to hearing from you!

Rae

Hi Maria,

My name is Summer Clarke and I am a visual artist based in Miami, Florida. I've been watching Artist 2 Artist on WXJK and I thought my perspective on typography could interest your audience.

I have been hand lettering and illustrating for a few years, with my work being used by local government and celebrities alike. Recently, I've been doing workshops on typography and I'd love to share this knowledge with your TV audience. I'll bring all the supplies and challenge your host to a 'typeoff'. It should be fun, interactive and of value to your aspiring artist audience.

Typography is quickly growing as one of the most recognized forms of art and I know we have a mutual interest in growing our local artistic community.

I've attached some resources for your perusal.

If we align, please feel free to contact me at 787.385.4938 or at this email address

Looking forward to hearing from you!

Summer

Hi Zayne,

My name is Jared Wales and I am a producer based in Miami, Florida. I would love to offer you an exclusive interview on my latest project, One Million Moons

This film is already being whispered about for Oscar buzz and the behind the scenes story of working with Tyler Cruz and Johnson Christian is one I bet your audience for Film Forward Entertainment would love. I would also be excited to share with your audience a trailer as well as a few unpublished behind the scenes shots and videos.

We know 2020 was a wild year and this feel deals with many of the feels that we've all felt when the days got darkest. I truly feel it will uplift anyone who sees it.

I've attached some resources for your perusal.

If we align, please feel free to contact me at 787.385.4938 or at this email address

Looking forward to hearing from you!

Jared

HEAP Practice Scenarios

Here are a few more HEAP Practice Scenarios to help you.

Instructions: Mix and match the following mediums, interview types and fictional scenarios to come up with a pitch. Don't forget your **HEAP.**

Medium	Scenario
Radio	**WildBeast Inc.** WildBeast Inc. is a dog training company for rescues that have particularly bad behavior issues
Television	**The Hummingbird Farm** The Hummingbird Farm is an outdoor space where patrons can feed several species of hummingbirds
Podcast	**Regenerative Face Therapy** You're a doctor that's just invented a brand new therapy that takes off years of aging
Newspaper Article	**Nailtrients Nail Co.** A nail polish company that promises to grow your nails from stubby to stiletto in 2 weeks
Instagram Live Interview	**The Baby Briar Band** You are the lead singer / songwriter of a band with new music out for the first time in 15 years

Blog	**Racie Shoes** You are a professional track athlete that has released a new line of shoes called Racie
Shot Live Talk Show	**Mermaid Mamas** A company that provides mermaids to entertain at children's birthday parties
Magazine Article	**Forensic Accounting Inc.** You are a forensic accountant specializing in million dollar divorces

Spotlight Starter Pack

With the permission or approval of the producer or showrunner, there are many ways to make your interview full of action and examples. Here are a few things to consider:

Game - Come up with some sort of game centered around your topic that the hosts can play with you. For example, as a coach demonstrating a fitness technique, you could challenge the hosts to a race and have a producer judge their form.

Quiz - Create a fun way to quiz your host or audience on what you've been talking about.

Leave a Challenge - Challenge viewers, readers or listeners after your interview slot, to some sort of activity or action such as logging on to a special page on your website for a prize

Demonstration - If you have a tangible product, definitely bring it with you if that is a possibility

Bring a Guest - Bring a guest to interact with or for demonstration purposes. For example, if you're a designer, you could ask if you could bring a model to wear your designs.

Videos, Photos and Other Media - Photos, videos, and any other pre-produced media can also be interactive and helpful

Visual Sites - Many websites exist where the audience can text in or log on to a URL and take a survey that gives you real time results. Even if you can't display them, at the end of your segment you can pull out your phone and read the results to further drive home interactivity and action.

Consider Music - If possible, reference music that aligns with your topic and then offer the playlist to viewers later on. This is a subtle but simple way to keep things interesting and get people to visit you afterwards

Pre-Interview Questions - Ask your existing clients, friends or audience to record or write in questions for you to answer live about your topic. If time allows, you can get to a few of them while in your interview. Of course, the advantage here is you can prep ahead of time.

Quick Reference:
Press Preparation Tips

- [ ] Research
- [ ] Ask Questions
- [ ] Decide your story and your examples
- [ ] Prepare for the pre-interview
- [ ] Have a statistic in your toolkit
- [ ] Practice in the mirror. Practice on a friend.
- [ ] Arrive Early
- [ ] Promote it
- [ ] Prepare your outfit
- [ ] Leave your devices (or at least really, truly silence them)

Quick Reference:
Prep ahead for surprise interviews

- ☐ Make sure you understand the outlet
- ☐ Give a short, concise statement
- ☐ Offer to follow up

Quick Reference:
Post Interview Checklist

- ☐ Say thank you
- ☐ Follow up and see when it will air
- ☐ Don't try to control the editing / article
- ☐ Share

Spotlight Style Basics

Here are 12 items to keep in your closet to mix and match so you're always ready for interviews:

- ☐ A classic Jean
- ☐ A solid pastel sweater, blouse or shirt
- ☐ A crisp button up
- ☐ A classic solid dress or dress shirt in navy blue or beige
- ☐ A mid-length wrap skirt
- ☐ A tailored blazer
- ☐ A basic cardigan
- ☐ A solid tie
- ☐ Tailored pants (black is okay)
- ☐ Plain ballet flats, sneakers, dress shoes or loafers
- ☐ A simple v-neck t-shirt
- ☐ An elegant watch

Interview Review Checklist

Here are a few things to look for when watching your interviews to make notes for improvement.

- ☐ How was my overall appearance?
- ☐ Did I have good eye contact?
- ☐ Did I come across with energy
- ☐ Was I slouching or hunched over?
- ☐ Did I react naturally and appropriately?
- ☐ Was my voice steady and my words clear?
- ☐ Did I get in my key message early?
- ☐ Was I rambling?
- ☐ Did I finish strong?
- ☐ Did I leave a way for the producers or audience to contact me?

Negative Press and Controversial Question Prompts

- *I can't discuss that now,* **but let me tell you something really fun…**
- *Everyone seems to be talking about that, so I don't blame you for asking,* **but there are so many things I'd love to tell you about away from that like…**
- *That's something I wonder to myself every day,* **but here's something I would love to answer**

It's a Wrap!

You made it! You're here! And even though I titled this 'it's a wrap', I only mean it's a wrap for this particular book. For you, your journey is just beginning. Remember, practice, practice, practice. Watch TV. Watch other interviews. Watch yourself. Don't forget that everyone started somewhere and even those who may have a natural gift for this still have to work at it. You may need to reference or quick reference the ideas in this book many times throughout your media journey, and maybe even read it again. Interviewing is an art and when the spotlight is on you, I'm 100% sure you'll be ready to shine.

XO,

Rae

Acknowledgements

There are so many people who have made not only this book a reality, but helped to turn my dreams and goals into the life I'm living today.

Firstly, I'd like to acknowledge Annette Tingle, the most phenomenal editor world over. This book was years in the making and without her push, sharp eye, words of encouragement, dedication, and personal belief in this book, this topic, and in me, this work would cease to be. Sadly, she is stuck with me for all subsequent books and adventures, but somehow I don't think she'll mind.

Thank you to Bobby Jones, for all his help and for access to many of the celebrities and opportunities that you read about in this book. This would not have been as colorful without you.

I am indebted to Anthony Miller and the entire crew of *Entertainment Report*. ER was my launch pad and many of the lessons I learned early and well were taught to me, directly or indirectly, by the phenomenal journalist and talent that is Anthony.

To the personalities who took the time to sit with me and grant me interviews specifically for these pages: Michael Yo, Xixi Yang, and Anya Ayoung-Chee, thank you so much for your time and sharing your expertise and talent. For the personalities I've encountered along the way who taught me something that I was able to use in this publication, thank you to you as well. My gratitude to Lyndsey McDonnough for supporting the early vision and allowing me to conduct the first set of workshops born from this vision, which helped to strengthen the book.

A special word of acknowledgement to my friends and family, especially those to whom this book is dedicated, for all of your encouragement and help. A listening ear and a friendly word went further than you could imagine on dark days.

And finally, to you, the person reading this book. For picking it up, for digesting my words, for your feedback, for your dedication to your craft and the enrichment of media as a whole, thanks a million! See you on future pages.

- Rae

About the Author

Raecine 'Rae' Williams is an entertainment journalist, TV host and media presence strategist who has been engaged in media industry since she was 9 years old. She is a world traveler, book lover and a teapot collector with a sweet tooth. Born and raised in Kingston, Jamaica, Rae now resides in Los Angeles, California with her two dogs Ivy and Quinn. She is a proud member of Alpha Kappa Alpha Sorority, Inc.

www.ingramcontent.com/pod-product-compliance
Lightning Source LLC
LaVergne TN
LVHW051557070426
835507LV00021B/2624